Morning
devotional

D. L. Moody

WHITAKER
HOUSE

Publisher's note:
D. L. Moody's selection of Bible versions has been retained
whenever possible, including the Revised Version (American
Edition) when it was originally cited. The text of this book,
however, has been updated for the modern reader. Words,
expressions, and sentence structure have been
revised for clarity and readability.

Unless otherwise indicated, all Scripture quotations are taken
from the King James Version (KJV) of the Holy Bible.
Scripture quotations marked (ASV) are from the American
Standard Edition of the Revised Version of the Holy Bible.

MORNING DEVOTIONAL

ISBN: 0-88368-718-6
Printed in the United States of America
© 1993 by Whitaker House

Whitaker House
30 Hunt Valley Circle
New Kensington, PA 15068
www.whitakerhouse.com

Library of Congress Cataloging-in-Publication Data

Moody, Dwight Lyman, 1837–1899.
Morning devotional / by D.L. Moody.
p.   cm.
ISBN 0-88368-718-6
1. Devotional calendars.   I. Title.
BV4811 .M56 2001
242'.2—dc21
2001004777

---

2 3 4 5 6 7 8 9 10 11 12 **ய** 11 10 09 08 07 06 05 04

C O N T E N T S

FOREWORD

One of the brightest signs of the times is that many Christian young people out in society and in church are observing a quiet hour daily. In this age of rushing and constant activity we need some special call to go apart and be alone with God for a part of each day. Any man or woman who does this faithfully and earnestly cannot be more than twenty-four hours away from God.

The selections given in this volume were first published in the monthly issues of the *Record of Christian Work,* Northfield, Massachusetts, and were found very helpful for devotional purposes. They are also a mine of thoughts, to illuminate the verses quoted. Being of permanent value, it has been thought desirable to transfer them from the pages of the magazine to this permanent volume.

May they have a helpful ministry, leading many into closer communion with God!

—D. L. MOODY

JANUARY

JANUARY 1

They shall mount up with wings as eagles;
they shall run, and not be weary;
and they shall walk, and not faint.
—Isaiah 40:31

This, my soul, is the triumph of your being—to be able to walk with God! Flight belongs to the young soul; it is the romance of religion. To run without weariness belongs to the lofty soul; it is the beauty of religion. But to walk and not faint belongs to the perfect soul; it is the power of religion.

Can you walk in white through the stained thoroughfares of men? Can you touch the vile and polluted ones of earth and retain your pure garments? Can you meet in contact with the sinful and be yourself undefiled? Then you have surpassed the flight of the eagle! —GEORGE MATHESON

JANUARY 2

Come up in the morning...and present thyself...to me
in the top of the mount.
—Exodus 34:2

My Father, I am coming. Nothing on the mean plain will keep me away from the holy heights. Help me to climb fast and keep my footing, lest I fall upon the hard rock! At Your bidding I come, so You will not mock my heart. Bring with You honey from heaven, yes, milk and wine, and oil for my soul's good, and stay the sun in its course, or the time will be too short in which to look upon Your face and to hear Your gentle voice.

Morning on the mount! It will make me strong and glad all the rest of the day so well begun.

—JOSEPH PARKER

JANUARY 3

My reward is with me.
—Revelation 22:12

We are to be rewarded, not only for work done, but for burdens borne; and I am not sure but that the brightest rewards will be for those who have borne burdens without murmuring. On that day He will take the lily that has been growing so long among thorns and lift it up to be the glory and wonder of all the universe, and the fragrance of that lily will draw forth ineffable praises from all the hosts of heaven.   —ANDREW BONAR

JANUARY 4

Where art thou?
—Genesis 3:9

Are you hiding yourself away from Him who would send you forth to do His own blessed work in His own way? Oh, let me say to you this morning, "The Lord has need of you." It may seem to be only a little thing He has for you to do, but it is an important one. He has "need of you." Do not turn your back upon Him; do not put yourself out of the way of being employed by Him. Do not begin by laying down laws for yourself as to what you will do and what you will not do, but cry out from the very depth of your heart, *"Here am I; send me"* (Isaiah 6:8). —W. HAY AITKEN

JANUARY 5

The Lord is my...song.
—Psalm 118:14

Let us think of God Himself becoming our song. This is the fullness and perfection of knowing God: to know Him so that He Himself becomes our delight; to know Him so that praise is sweetest and fullest and freshest and gladdest, when we sing of Him. He who has learned this blessed secret carries the golden key of heaven—no, he has fetched heaven down to earth and need not envy the angels now. —MARK GUY PEARSE

JANUARY 6

Many are the afflictions of the righteous: but the LORD
delivereth him out of them all.
—Psalm 34:19

All the afflictions of the righteous open out into something glorious. The prisoner is not merely delivered, but he finds an angel waiting for him at the door. And with every deliverance comes a specific blessing. One angel is named faith; another, love; another, joy; another, longsuffering; another, gentleness; another, goodness; another, meekness; another, temperance; and another, peace. Each of these graces says, "We came out of great tribulation." (See Revelation 7:14.)   —G. BOWEN

JANUARY 7

Take good heed therefore unto yourselves.
—Joshua 23:11

Gold cannot be used for currency as long as it is mixed with the quartz and rock in which it lies imbedded. So your soul is useless to God until taken out from sin and earthliness and selfishness, in which it lies buried. By the regenerating power of the Spirit, you must be separated unto Christ, stamped with His image and superscription, and made into a divine currency, which will bear His likeness among men. The Christian is, so to speak, the circulating medium of Christ, the coin of the realm by whom the great transactions of mercy and grace to a lost world are carried on. As the currency stands for the gold, so does the Christian stand for Christ, representing His good and acceptable will. —A. J. GORDON

JANUARY 8

Count it all joy when ye fall into divers temptations.
—James 1:2

We cannot be losers by trusting God, for He is honored by faith, and most honored when faith discerns His love and truth behind a thick cloud of His ways and providence. Happy are those who are thus tried! Let us only be clear of unbelief and a guilty conscience. We will hide ourselves in the rock and pavilion of the Lord, sheltered beneath the wings of everlasting love until all calamities be overpassed.　　　　　　—SELECTED

JANUARY 9

Moses was in the mount forty days and forty nights.
—Exodus 24:18

The life of fellowship with God cannot be built up in a day. It begins with the habitual reference of all to Him, hour by hour, as Moses did in Egypt. But it moves on to more and longer periods of communion, and it finds its consummation and bliss in days and nights of intercession and waiting and holy conversation.　　　　　　—F. B. MEYER

JANUARY 10

Under his shadow.
—Song of Solomon 2:3

I seem to see four pictures suggested by that: under the shadow of a rock in a weary plain; under the shadow of a tree; closer still, under the shadow of His wing; nearest and closest, in the shadow of His hand. Surely that hand must be the pierced hand, that may oftentimes press us sorely, and yet be evermore encircling, upholding, and shadowing!

—FRANCES RIDLEY HAVERGAL

JANUARY 11

My voice shalt thou hear in the morning, O Lord; in the morning will I direct my prayer unto thee, and will look up.
—Psalm 5:3

The morning is the gate of the day, and should be well-guarded with prayer. It is one end of the thread on which the day's actions are strung, and should be well-knotted with devotion. If we felt more the majesty of life we would be more careful of its mornings. He who rushes from his bed to his business and does not wait to worship is as foolish as if he had not put on his clothes or cleansed his face, and as unwise as if he dashed into battle without arms or armor. It is ours to bathe in the softly flowing river of communion with God, before the

14

heat of the wilderness and the burden of the way begin to oppress us. —SPURGEON

JANUARY 12

He made as though he would have gone further.
—Luke 24:28

Is not God always acting thus? He comes to us by His Holy Spirit as He did to these two disciples. He speaks to us through the preaching of the Gospel, through the Word of God, through the various means of grace and the providential circumstances of life; and having thus spoken, He makes as though He would go further. If the ear is opened to His voice and the heart to His Spirit, the prayer will then go up, "Lord, abide with me." But if that voice makes no impression, then He passes on, as He has done thousands of times, leaving the heart at each time harder than before, and the ear more closed to the Spirit's call. —F. WHITFIELD

JANUARY 13

Christ is all, and in all.
—Colossians 3:11

The *service* of Christ is the *business* of my life.
The *will* of Christ is the *law* of my life.
The *presence* of Christ is the *joy* of my life.
The *glory* of Christ is the *crown* of my life.
—AUTHOR UNKNOWN

JANUARY 14

Herein is my Father glorified, that ye bear much fruit.
—John 15:8

What a possibility, what an inspiration, that we can enhance the glory of our Father! Our hearts leap at the thought. How can this be done? By bearing "leaves"—a profession of love for Him? No. By bearing some fruit? No. *"That you bear much fruit."* In the abundance of the yield is the joy, the glory of the husbandman. We should, therefore, aim to be extraordinary, "hundredfold" Christians, satisfied with nothing but the largest yield. Our lives should be packed with good deeds. Then at harvest time we will be able to say, "Father, I have glorified You on the earth!" (See John 17:4.)

—W. JENNINGS

JANUARY 15

Blessed are they that have not seen,
and yet have believed.
—John 20:29

The seen are shadows: the substance is found in the unseen. No doubt, in Christ, the foundation of our faith is unseen; but so is that of yonder tower that lifts its tall, erect form among the waves over which it throws a saving light. It appears to rest on the rolling billows, but beneath these, invisible and immovable lies the solid rock on which it stands secure. And when the hurricane roars above, and breakers roar below, I could go calmly to sleep in that lone sea tower. Founded on a rock, and safer than the proudest palace that stands on the sandy, surf-beaten shore, it cannot be moved. Still less the Rock of Ages! Whoever trusts in that is fit for death, prepared for judgment, ready for the last day's sounding trumpet, since *"the LORD redeemeth the soul of his servants: and none of them that trust in him shall be desolate"* (Psalm 34:22).

—GUTHRIE

JANUARY 16

My God shall be my strength.
—Isaiah 49:5

Oh, do not pray for easy lives! Pray to be stronger men! Do not pray for tasks equal to your powers; pray for powers equal to your tasks! Then the doing of your work will not be a miracle, but you will be a miracle. Every day you will wonder at yourself, at the richness of life that has come into you by the grace of God.　　　　—PHILLIPS BROOKS

JANUARY 17

Not as I will, but as thou wilt.
—Matthew 26:39

There are no disappointments to those whose wills are buried in the will of God.　　　　—FABER

JANUARY 18

Therefore we are buried with him by baptism into death: that like as Christ was raised up from the dead by the glory of the Father, even so we also should walk in newness of life.
—Romans 6:4

That is the life we are called on to live, and that is the life it is our privilege to lead; for God never gives us a call without it being a privilege, and He never gives us the privilege to come up higher without stretching out to us His hand to lift us up. Come up higher and higher into the realities and glories of the resurrection life, knowing that your life is *"hid with Christ in God"* (Colossians 3:3). Shake yourself loose of every encumbrance, turn your back on every defilement, give yourself over like clay to the hands of the Potter, so that He may stamp upon you the fullness of His own resurrection glory, that you, beholding as in a mirror the glory of the Lord, may be changed from glory to glory as by the Spirit of the Lord. (See 2 Corinthians 3:18.)   —W. HAY AITKEN

JANUARY 19

Now are ye light in the Lord: walk as children of light.
—Ephesians 5:8

The influence we exert in the world is created by our relationship to Jesus Christ; and our relationship to Christ is revealed by our influence.
—SELECTED

JANUARY 20

Thou shalt make holy garments for Aaron.
—Exodus 28:2

Have we no garments of blue, purple, and beautiful suggestiveness? We have garments of praise; we are clothed with the Lord Jesus. Have we no ornaments? The ornament of a meek and quiet spirit is, in the sight of God, of great price. Have we no golden bells? We have the golden bells of holy actions. Our words, our actions, and our purposes are bells. Wherever we move, our motion is thus understood to be a motion toward holy places, holy deeds, and holy character.   —JOSEPH PARKER

JANUARY 21

My God shall supply all your need according to his riches in glory by Christ Jesus.
—Philippians 4:19

What a source—*"God"*! What a standard—*"His riches in glory"*! What a channel—*"Christ Jesus"*! It is your sweet privilege to place all your needs in contrast with His riches, and lose sight of the former in the presence of the latter. His exhaustless treasury is thrown open to you, in all the love of His heart; go and draw upon it, in the artless simplicity of faith, and you will never have occasion to look to a creature-stream, or lean on a creature-prop.
—C. H. M

JANUARY 22

There remaineth therefore a rest to the people of God.
—Hebrews 4:9

How sweet the music of this heavenly chime is, floating across the waters of death from the towers of the New Jerusalem. Pilgrim, fainting under your long and arduous pilgrimage, hear it! It is *"rest."* Soldier, carrying still the blood and dust of battle, hear it! It is *"rest."* Voyager, tossed on the waves of sin and sorrow, driven here and there on the world's heaving ocean of vicissitude, hear it! The haven is in sight; the very waves that are breaking on you murmur, "So He gives His beloved rest."

The long-drawn sigh of existence at last is answered. The toil and travail of earth's protracted week is at an end. The calm of its unbroken Sabbath is begun. Weary man has found at last the long-sought for rest in the bosom of his God!

—MACDUFF

JANUARY 23

Despising the shame.
—Hebrews 12:2

And how is that to be done? In two ways. Go up the mountain, and the things in the plain will look very small; the higher you rise, the more insignificant they will seem. Hold fellowship with God, and the threatening foes here will seem very, very unformidable. Another way is to pull up the curtain and gaze on what is behind it. The low foothills that lie at the base of some Alpine country may look high when seen from the plain, as long as the snowy summits are wrapped in mist; but when a little puff of wind comes and clears away the fog from the lofty peaks, nobody looks at the little green hills in front. So the world's hindrances and the world's difficulties and cares look very lofty until the cloud lifts. But when we see the great white summits, everything lower does not seem so very high after all. Look to Jesus and that will dwarf the difficulties.

—ALEXANDER MACLAREN

JANUARY 24

He that is faithful in that which is least is faithful
also in much.
—Luke 16:10

The least action of life can be as surely done from the loftiest motive as the highest and noblest acts. Faithfulness measures acts as God measures them. True conscientiousness deals with our duties as God deals with them. Duty is duty, conscience is conscience, right is right, and wrong is wrong, whatever sized type they are printed in. Large and small are not words for the vocabulary of conscience. It knows only two words—right and wrong.

—ALEXANDER MACLAREN

JANUARY 25

Show me thy ways, O LORD; teach me thy paths.
—Psalm 25:4

There is a path in which every child of God is to walk, and in which alone God can accompany him.
—DENHAM SMITH

JANUARY 26

And Elisha...said, LORD, I pray thee, open his eyes, that he may see.
—2 Kings 6:17

This is the prayer we need to pray for ourselves and for one another, "Lord, open our eyes that we may see"; for the world all around us, as well as around the prophet, is full of God's horses and chariots, waiting to carry us to places of glorious victory. And when our eyes are thus opened, we will see in all the events of life, whether great or small, whether joyful or sad, a "chariot" for our souls. Everything that comes to us becomes a chariot the moment we treat it as such; and, on the other hand, even the smallest trial may be a juggernaut to crush us into misery or despair if we consider them so. It lies with each of us to choose which they will be. It all depends, not upon what these events are, but upon how we take them. If we lie down under them and let them roll over us and crush us, they become juggernauts, but if we climb up into them, as into a car of victory, and make them carry us triumphantly onward and upward, they become the chariots of God. —SMITH

JANUARY 27

The living God.
—Daniel 6:20

How many times we find this expression in the Scriptures, and yet it is just this very thing that we are so prone to lose sight of! We know it is written *"the living God"*; but in our daily life there is scarcely anything we lose sight of so much as the fact that God is *the living God;* that He is now whatever He was three or four thousand years ago; that He has the same sovereign power, the same saving love toward those who love and serve Him as ever He had, and that He will do for them now what He did for others two, three, four thousand years ago, simply because He is *"the living God,"* the Unchanging One. Oh, how we should confide in Him therefore, and in our darkest moments never lose sight of the fact that He is still and ever will be *"the living God."* —GEORGE MUELLER

JANUARY 28

Are there not twelve hours in the day?
—John 11:9

The very fact of a Christian being here, and not in heaven, is a proof that some work awaits him.
—WILLIAM ARNOT

JANUARY 29

Fear ye not, stand still, and see
the salvation of the Lord.
—Exodus 14:13

Often God seems to place His children in positions of profound difficulty, leading them into a wedge from which there is no escape, contriving a situation that no human judgment would have permitted had it been previously consulted. The very cloud conducts them there. You may be thus involved at this very hour. It does seem perplexing and very serious to the last degree, but it is perfectly right. The issue will more than justify Him who has brought you here. It is a platform for the display of His almighty grace and power. He will not only deliver you, but in doing so He will give you a lesson that you will never forget; and to which, in many a psalm and song in later days, you will revert. You will never be able to thank God enough for having done just as He has.   —F. B. MEYER

JANUARY 30

All things work together for good to them that love God.
—Romans 8:28

In one thousand trials it is not five hundred of them that work for the believer's good, but nine hundred and ninety-nine of them, and one beside.

—GEORGE MUELLER

JANUARY 31

Every day will I bless thee; and I will praise
thy name for ever and ever.
—Psalm 145:2

There is a very beautiful device by which the Japanese are accustomed to express their wishes for their friends. It is the figure of a drum in which the birds have built their nest. The story told of it is that once there lived a good king, so anxiously concerned for the welfare of his people that at the palace gate he set a drum, and whoever had any wrong to be redressed, or any want, should beat the drum, and at once, by day or night, the king would grant the supplicant an audience and relief. But throughout the land there reigned such prosperity and contentment that none needed to appeal for anything, and the birds built their nests within it and filled it with the music of their song.

Such gracious access is granted to us even by the King of heaven, and day and night His ready hearing and His help are within the reach of all who come to Him; but of all men, most blessed are they who have found on earth a blessedness in which all want is forgotten, and trust rests so assured of safety in the Father's care that prayer gives place to ceaseless praise. They rejoice in the Lord always. —MARK GUY PEARSE

F E B R U A R Y

FEBRUARY 1

Love not the world.
—1 John 2:15

Love it not, and yet love it. Love it with the love of Him who gave His Son to die for it. Love it with the love of Him who shed His blood for it. Love it with the love of angels who rejoice in its conversion. Love it to do it good, giving your tears to its sufferings, your pity to its sorrows, your wealth to its wants, your prayers to its miseries, and to its fields of charity and philanthropy and Christian piety your powers and hours of labor. You cannot live without affecting it or being affected by it. You will make the world better, or it will make you worse. God help you by His grace and Holy Spirit so to live in the world as to live above it and look beyond it; and so to love it that when you leave it, you may leave it better than you found it.

—GUTHRIE

FEBRUARY 2

Continue in prayer.
—Colossians 4:2

Do you want nothing? Then I fear you do not know your poverty. Have you no mercy to ask of God? Then may the Lord's mercy show you your misery. A prayerless soul is a Christless soul. Prayer is the lisping of the believing infant, the shout of the fighting believer, and the requiem of the dying saint falling asleep in Jesus. —SPURGEON

FEBRUARY 3

In whom all the building fitly framed together groweth unto an holy temple in the Lord.
—Ephesians 2:21

The life-tabernacle is a wondrous building; there is room for workers of all kinds in the uprearing of its mysterious and glorious walls. If we cannot do the greatest work, we may do the least. Our heaven will come out of the realization of the fact that it was God's tabernacle we were building, and under God's blessing that we were working.
—JOSEPH PARKER

FEBRUARY 4

By faith Abraham, when he was called to go out into a place which he should after

receive for an inheritance, obeyed.
—Hebrews 11:8

Where he went, he knew not; it was enough for him to know that he went with God. He leaned not so much upon the promises as upon the Promiser. He did not look on the difficulties of his lot, but on *"the King eternal, immortal, invisible, the only wise God"* (1 Timothy 1:17), who had deigned to appoint his course, and would certainly vindicate Himself. O glorious faith! This is your work, and these are your possibilities: contentment to sail with sealed orders, because of unwavering confidence in the love and wisdom of the Lord High Admiral; willingness to rise up, leave all, and follow Christ, because of the glad assurance that earth's best cannot bear comparison with heaven's least.

—F. B. MEYER

FEBRUARY 5

Thou openest thine hand, and satisfiest the desire of every living thing.
—Psalm 145:16

Desire, it is a dainty word! It was much that He would satisfy the need, the want; but He goes far beyond that. Pity is moved to meet our need; duty may sometimes look after our wants, but to satisfy the desire implies a tender watchfulness, a sweet and gracious knowledge of us, an eagerness of blessing. God is never satisfied until He has satisfied our desires.   —MARK GUY PEARSE

FEBRUARY 6

Ye servants of the LORD, which by night stand in the house of the LORD....The LORD that made heaven and earth bless thee out of Zion.
—Psalm 134:1, 3

If I would know the love of my friend, I must see what it can do in the winter. So with the divine love. It is very easy for me to worship in the summer sunshine, when the melodies of life are in the air and the fruits of life are on the tree. But let the song of the bird cease and the fruit of the tree fall, and will my heart still go on to sing? Will I stand in God's house by night? Will I love Him in His own night? Will I watch Him even one hour in His Gethsemane? Will I help to bear His cross up the *via dolorosa?* My love has come to Him in His humiliation. My faith has found Him in His lowliness. My heart has recognized His majesty through His mean disguise, and I know at last that I do not desire the gift, but the Giver. When I can stand in His house by night, I have accepted Him for Himself alone. —GEORGE MATHESON

FEBRUARY 7

He loveth our nation, and he hath built us a synagogue.
—Luke 7:5

Marble and granite are perishable monuments, and their inscriptions may be seldom read. Carve

your names on human hearts; they alone are
immortal!   —THEODORE CUYLER

FEBRUARY 8

*Get thee out of thy country, and from thy kindred, and
from thy father's house.*
—Genesis 12:1

Abraham...was gathered to his people.
—Genesis 25:8

After all communion, we dwell as upon
islands, dotted over a great archipelago, each
upon his little rock with the sea dashing between
us; but the time comes when, if our hearts are
set upon that great Lord whose presence makes
us one, there will be no more sea, and all the iso-
lated rocks will be parts of a great continent. If
we cultivate that sense of detachment from the
present and of having our true affinities in the
unseen, if we dwell here as strangers because our
citizenship is in heaven, then death will not drag
us away from our associates nor hunt us into a
lonely land, but will bring us where closer bonds
will knit the "sweet societies" together, and the
sheep will couch close by one another because
all gathered round the one Shepherd. Then many
ties will be rewoven, and the solitary wanderer
will meet again the dear ones whom he had
"loved long since and lost awhile."
—ALEXANDER MACLAREN

FEBRUARY 9

*At the commandment of the LORD they rested
in the tents, and at the commandment
of the LORD they journeyed.*
—Numbers 9:23

This is the secret of peace and calm elevation. If an Israelite in the desert had taken it into his head to make some movement independent of Jehovah, if he took it upon himself to move when the crowd was at rest or to halt while the crowd was moving, we can easily see what the result would have been. So it will ever be with us. If we move when we ought to rest, or rest when we ought to move, we will not have the divine presence with us.

—C. H. M.

FEBRUARY 10

Then shall we know, if we follow on to know the LORD.
—Hosea 6:3

The Lord has brought us into the pathway of the knowledge of Him, and bids us to pursue that path through all its strange meanderings until it opens out upon the plain where God's throne is. Our life is a following on to know the Lord. We marvel at some of the experiences through which we are called to pass, but afterward we see that they afforded us some new knowledge of our Lord. We do not have to wait for some brighter opportunity, but by improvement of the present are to build for ourselves a bridge to that future.   —G. BOWEN

FEBRUARY 11

As many as I love, I...chasten.
—Revelation 3:19

I once saw a dark shadow resting on the bare side of a hill. Seeking its cause, I saw a little cloud, bright as the light, floating in the clear blue above. Thus it is with our sorrow. It may be dark and cheerless here on earth, yet look above and you will see it to be but a shadow of His brightness whose name is Love.   —DEAN ALFORD

FEBRUARY 12

Therefore will the LORD wait, that he may be gracious unto you.
—Isaiah 30:18

This is God's way. In the darkest hours of the night, His tread draws near across the billows. As the day of execution is breaking, the angel comes to Peter's cell. When the scaffold for Mordecai is complete, the royal sleeplessness leads to a reaction in favor of the threatened race. Ah, soul, it may have come to the worst with you before you are delivered; but you will be! God may keep you waiting, but He will be ever mindful of His covenant, and will appear to fulfill His inviolable word.   —F. B. MEYER

FEBRUARY 13

*He that saith he abideth in him ought himself also so
to walk, even as he walked.*
—1 John 2:6

The preaching that this world needs most is
the sermons in shoes that are walking with Jesus
Christ. —SELECTED

FEBRUARY 14

*In whom also after that ye believed, ye were sealed
with that holy Spirit of promise.*
—Ephesians 1:13

The Lord puts a seal upon His own, that every-
body may know them. The sealing in your case is
the Spirit producing in you likeness to the Lord.
The holier you become, the more distinct and plain,
the more evident to every passerby, the seal is, for
then men will take knowledge of you that you have
been with Jesus. —ANDREW BONAR

FEBRUARY 15

Jacob went on his way, and the angels of God met him.
—Genesis 32:1

In the path where God has entreated us to walk,
we will find the angels around us. We may meet
them, indeed, on paths of our own choosing, but

it will be the sort of angel that Balaam met, with a sword in his hand, mighty and beautiful, but wrathful too; and we had better not confront him! But the friendly helpers, the emissaries of God's love, the apostles of His grace, do not haunt the roads that we make for ourselves.   —ALEXANDER MACLAREN

FEBRUARY 16

To every man his work.
—Mark 13:34

He does the most for God's great world who does the best in his own little world.   —SELECTED

FEBRUARY 17

I will help thee, saith the LORD.
—Isaiah 41:14

O my soul, is not this enough? Do you need more strength than the omnipotence of the united Trinity? Do you want more wisdom than exists in the Father, more love than displays itself in the Son, or more power than is manifest in the influences of the Spirit? Bring here your empty pitcher! Surely this well will fill it. Haste, gather up your wants, and bring them here—your emptiness, your woes, your needs. Behold, this river of God is full for your supply; what can you desire beside? Go forth, my soul, in this your might. The eternal God is your helper!   —SPURGEON

FEBRUARY 18

Boast not thyself of to morrow.
—Proverbs 27:1

The only preparation for tomorrow is the right use of today. The stone in the hands of the builder must be put in its place and fitted to receive another. The morrow comes to nothing if today is not heeded. Do not neglect the call that comes to you this day, for such neglect is nothing else than boasting yourself of tomorrow.　　　—G. BOWEN

FEBRUARY 19

What mean these stones?
—Joshua 4:21

Ye also, as lively stones.
—1 Peter 2:5

There should be something so remarkable, so special about the life and conversation of a Christian that men should be compelled to ask, "What does this mean?" Is there anything in your character, words, and habits of life so different from the world around you that men are involuntarily compelled to ask themselves or others, "What does this mean?" Not that there is to be a forced singularity, a peculiarity for the sake of being peculiar; that would merely be to copy the pharisaism of ancient days. Oh, that we might realize that this is the purpose for which God sends us into the world, as He sent His only begotten Son!

—S. A. BLACKWOOD

FEBRUARY 20

Philip findeth Nathanael, and saith unto him, We have found him, of whom Moses in the law, and the prophets, did write....Come and see.
—John 1:45–46

The next thing to knowing that *"we have found him"* is to find someone else, and say, *"Come and see."* —FRANCES RIDLEY HAVERGAL

FEBRUARY 21

The wind bloweth where it listeth, and thou hearest the sound thereof, but canst not tell whence it cometh, and whither it goeth: so is every one that is born of the Spirit.
—John 3:8

We know that the wind lists to blow where there is a vacuum. If you find a tremendous rush of wind, you know that somewhere there is an empty space. I am perfectly sure about this fact: if we could expel all pride, vanity, self-righteousness, self-seeking, desire for applause, honor, and promotion—if by some divine power we would be utterly emptied of all that—the Spirit would come as a rushing mighty wind to fill us. —A. J. GORDON

FEBRUARY 22

The Lord is a God of knowledge,
and by him actions are weighed.
—1 Samuel 2:3

God does not measure what we bring to Him. He weighs it. —MARK GUY PEARSE

FEBRUARY 23

All...saw his face as it had been the face of an angel.
—Acts 6:15

The face is made every day by its morning prayer, and by its morning look out of windows that open upon heaven. —JOSEPH PARKER

FEBRUARY 24

After ye were illuminated, ye endured
a great fight of afflictions.
—Hebrews 10:32

Our boldness for God before the world must always be the result of individual dealing with God in secret. Our victories over self, sin, and the world are always first fought where no eye sees but God's. If we do not have these secret conflicts, we may well not have any open ones. The outward absence of conflict betrays the inward sleep of the soul.

—F. WHITFIELD

FEBRUARY 25

*I am the way, the truth, and the life: no man cometh
unto the Father, but by me.*
—John 14:6

Heaven often seems distant and unknown, but if He who made the road there is our guide, we need not fear to lose the way. We do not want to see far ahead—only far enough to discern Him and trace His footsteps. They who follow Christ, even through darkness, will surely reach the Father.

—HENRY VAN DYKE

FEBRUARY 26

*Forgetting those things which are behind...
I press toward the mark for the prize
of the high calling of God in Christ Jesus.*
—Philippians 3:13–14

It is not by regretting what is irreparable that true work is to be done, but by making the best of what we are. It is not by complaining that we do not have the right tools, but by using well the tools we have. What we are and where we are is God's providential arrangement—God's doing—though it may be man's misdoing. Life is a series of mistakes, and he who makes the fewest false steps is not the best Christian. He who wins the most splendid victories by the retrieval of mistakes is the best.

—F. W. ROBERTSON

FEBRUARY 27

Thy gentleness hath made me great.
—2 Samuel 22:36

The gentleness of Christ is the comeliest ornament that a Christian can wear. —WILLIAM ARNOT

FEBRUARY 28

Bring of the fish which ye have now caught.
—John 21:10

Why was this? Oh, the Lord wants us to minister to Him as well as to receive from Him, and our service finds its true end when it becomes food for our dear Lord. He was pleased to feed on their fish while they were feeding on His. It was the double banquet of which He speaks in the tender message of revelation, *"I...will sup with him, and he with me"* (Revelation 3:20). —A. B. SIMPSON

M A R C H

MARCH 1

As captain of the host of the LORD am I now come.
—Joshua 5:14

Surely, Israel might now face the foe with unwavering confidence and sing of victory even before the battle was gained. And so may the Christian. He does not advance to a conflict of uncertain issue; the result of the battle is not doubtful. The struggle may be severe, the warfare long; he may sometimes, like the pilgrim, be beaten to the ground, and well-nigh lose his sword; but though *"cast down,"* he is *"not destroyed"* (2 Corinthians 4:9). The Captain of salvation is on his side, and in the midst of sharpest conflict he can say, "Thanks be unto God, who gives us the victory through our Lord Jesus Christ" (1 Corinthians 15:57).

—S. A. BLACKWOOD

MARCH 2

Whatsoever a man soweth, that shall he also reap.
—Galatians 6:7

The most common actions of life, its every day and hour, are invested with the highest grandeur, when we think how they extend their issues into eternity. Our hands are now sowing seeds for that great harvest. We will meet again all we are doing and have done. The graves will give up their dead, and from the tombs of oblivion the past will give up all that it holds in keeping, to bear true witness for or against us.   —GUTHRIE

MARCH 3

When he cometh into the world, he saith,...a body hast thou prepared me.
—Hebrews 10:5

The word of Christ must be adopted by each of His followers. Nothing will help us to live in this world and keep ourselves unspotted but the Spirit that was in Christ, that looked upon His body as prepared by God for His service; that looks upon our bodies as prepared by Him too, that we might offer them to Him. Like Christ, we too have a body in which the Holy Spirit dwells. Like Christ, we too must yield our bodies, with every member, every power, every action, to fulfill His will, to be offered up to Him, to glorify Him. Like Christ, we must prove in our bodies that we are holy to the Lord. —ANDREW MURRAY

MARCH 4

He that abideth in me, and I in him, the same bringeth forth much fruit: for without me ye can do nothing.
—John 15:5

Too much taken up with our work, we may forget our Master. It is possible to have the hand full, and the heart empty. Taken up with our Master, we cannot forget our work. If the heart is filled with His love, how can the hands not be active in His service? —ADOLPHE MONOD

MARCH 5

He leadeth me in the paths of righteousness for his name's sake.
—Psalm 23:3

He always has a purpose in His leading. He knows where the bits of green pasture are, and He would lead His flock to these. The way may be rough, but it is the right way to the pasture. *"Paths of righteousness"* may not be straight paths; but they are paths that lead somewhere—to the right place. Many desert paths are illusive. They start out clear and plain, but soon they are lost in the sands. They go nowhere. But the paths of righteousness have a goal to which they unerringly lead. —J. R. MILLER

MARCH 6

*There are eleven days' journey from Horeb by the
way of mount Seir unto Kadeshbarnea.*
—Deuteronomy 1:2

Eleven days, and yet it took them forty years! How
was this? Alas, we need not travel far for the answer.
It is only too like ourselves. How slowly we get over
the ground! What windings and turnings! How often
we have to go back and travel over the same ground,
again and again. We are slow travelers because we are
slow learners. Our God is a faithful and wise, as well
as a gracious and patient Teacher. He will not permit
us to pass cursorily over our lessons. Sometimes, perhaps, we think we have mastered a lesson, and we
attempt to move on to another, but our wise Teacher
knows better, and He sees the need of deeper plow-
ing. He will not have us mere theorists or smatterers;
He will keep us, if need be, year after year at our
scales until we learn to sing.   —C. H. M.

MARCH 7

The children of your Father which is in heaven.
—Matthew 5:45

The best name by which we can think of God is
"Father." It is a loving, deep, sweet, heart-touching
name, for the name of father is in its nature full of
inborn sweetness and comfort. Therefore, also, we
must confess ourselves children of God, for by this

name we deeply touch our God, since there is not a sweeter sound to the father than the voice of the child. —MARTIN LUTHER

MARCH 8

If we confess our sins, he is faithful and just to forgive us our sins, and to cleanse us from all unrighteousness.
—1 John 1:9

The same moment that brings the consciousness of sin ought to bring also the confession of it and the consciousness of forgiveness. —SMITH

MARCH 9

Full of [satisfied with] *years.*
—Genesis 25:8

Scaffoldings are for buildings, and the moments and days and years of our earthly lives are scaffolding. What are you building inside it? What kind of a structure will be disclosed when the scaffolding is knocked away? Days and years are ours, that they may give us what eternity cannot take away—a character built upon the love of God in Christ, and molded into His likeness. Has your life helped you to do that? If so, you have gotten the best out of it, and your life is completed, whatever the number of its days may be. Quality, not quantity, is the thing that determines the perfectness of a life. Does your life have this completeness? —ALEXANDER MACLAREN

MARCH 10

Keep yourselves in the love of God.
—Jude 21

Fruit ripened in the sun is sweetest.
—SELECTED

MARCH 11

Beautiful

I sought him, but I found him not.
—Song of Solomon 3:1

Tell me where you lost the company of Christ, and I will tell you the most likely place to find Him. Have you lost Christ in the closet by restraining prayer? Then it is there you must seek and find Him. Did you lose Christ by sin? You will find Him in no other way than by giving up the sin, and seeking by the Holy Spirit to mortify the member in which the lust dwells. Did you lose Christ by neglecting the Scriptures? You must find Him in the Scriptures. It is a true proverb, "Look for a thing where you dropped it; it is there." So look for Christ where you lost Him, for He has not gone away.   —SPURGEON

MARCH 12

Come up in the morning...and present thyself there to me in the top of the mount.
—Exodus 34:2

The morning is the time fixed for my meeting the Lord. This very word *morning* is as a cluster of rich grapes. Let me crush them and drink the sacred wine.

"In the morning"! Then God means me to be at my best in strength and hope. I do not have to climb in my weakness. In the night I have buried yesterday's fatigue, and in the morning I take a new lease of energy.

Sweet morning! There is hope in its music. Blessed is the day whose morning is sanctified! Successful is the day whose first victory was won in prayer! Holy is the day whose dawn finds you on the top of the mount! Health is established in the morning. Wealth is won in the morning. The light is brightest *"in the morning." "Awake, psaltery and harp: I myself will awake early"* (Psalm 57:8).

—JOSEPH PARKER

MARCH 13

He that eateth me, even he shall live by me.
—John 6:57

To feed on Christ is to get His strength into us to be our strength. You feed on the cornfield, and the strength of the cornfield comes into you, and is your strength. You feed on Christ, and then go and live your life. And it is Christ in you who lives your life, who helps the poor, who tells the truth, who fights the battles, and who wins the crown.

—PHILLIPS BROOKS

MARCH 14

Ye shall receive power, after that the Holy Ghost is
come upon you: and ye shall be witnesses unto me.
—Acts 1:8

Look at it! Think of it! A hundred and twenty
men and women having no patronage, no promise of
any earthly favor, no endowment, no wealth—a company of men and women having to get their living by
common daily toil, and busied with all the household
duties of daily life—and yet they are to begin the conquest of Christianity! A work that is to turn the world
upside down is entrusted to them. No one so exalted
that the influence of this lowly company will not reach
them, until the throne of the Caesars is claimed for
Christ. No one is so far off that the power of this little
band gathered in an upper room will not extend to
them until the whole world is knit into a brotherhood!
There is not a force on the earth, either of men or
devils, that they will not overcome, until every knee
will bow to their Master, and every tongue will confess that He is Lord. (See Philippians 2:10–11).

A thing impossible, absurd, look at it as you will,
until you admit this—they are to be filled with the
Holy Spirit. Then difficulties melt into the empty air.
Then there is no limit to their hopes, for there is no
limit to their power. Their strength is not only "as the
strength of ten," it is as the strength of the Almighty.

This is Christ's idea of Christianity; the idea
not of man—it is infinitely too sublime—the idea of
God!   —MARK GUY PEARSE

48

MARCH 15

To me to live is Christ, and to die is gain.
—Philippians 1:21

Live in Christ, and you are in the suburbs of heaven. There is but a thin wall between you and the land of praises. You are within one hour's sailing of the shore of the new Canaan.
—WILLIAM RUTHERFORD

MARCH 16

Quench not the Spirit.
—1 Thessalonians 5:19

In order that you may not quench the Spirit, you must make it a constant study to know what the mind of the Spirit is. You must discriminate with the utmost care between His suggestions and the suggestions of your own deceitful heart. You will keep in constant recollection what the offices of the Spirit are as described by Christ in the gospel of John. You will be on your guard against impulsive movements, inconsiderate acts, and rash words. You will abide in prayer. Search the Word. Confess Christ on all possible occasions. Seek the society of His people. Shrink from conformity to the world, its vain fashions, and unmeaning etiquette. Be scrupulous in your reading. *"What I say unto you I say unto all, Watch"* (Mark 13:37). "Have oil in your lamps." (See Matthew 25:1–13). *"Quench not the Spirit."*
—BOWEN

MARCH 17

And he said, O my Lord, send, I pray thee, by the hand
of him whom thou wilt send.
—Exodus 4:13

It was a very grudging assent. It was as much as to say, "Since you are determined to send me and I must undertake the mission, then let it be so; but I would that it might have been another, and I go because I am compelled." So often do we shrink back from the sacrifice or obligation to which God calls us, that we think we are going to our doom. We seek every reason for evading the divine will, little realizing that He is forcing us out from our quiet homes into a career that includes, among other things, the song of victory on the banks of the Red Sea, the two lonely sojourns for forty days in converse with God, the shining face, the vision of glory, the burial by the hand of Michael, and the supreme honor of standing beside the Lord on the transfiguration mount.   —F. B. MEYER

MARCH 18

Take us the foxes, the little foxes, that spoil the
vineyards; for our vineyards are in blossom.
—Song of Solomon 2:15 ASV

How numerous the little foxes are! Little compromises with the world; disobedience to the still, small voice in little things; little indulgences to the flesh to the neglect of duty; little strokes of policy; doing evil in little things that good may come. With them, the beauty and fruitfulness of the vine are sacrificed! —J. HUDSON TAYLOR

MARCH 19

Come behind in no gift.
—1 Corinthians 1:7

The Scripture gives four names to Christians, taken from the four cardinal graces so essential to man's salvation: saints for their holiness, believers for their faith, brethren for their love, disciples for their knowledge. —THOMAS FULLER

MARCH 20

Bear ye one another's burdens, and so fulfil the law of Christ.
—Galatians 6:2

By lifting the burdens of others, we lose our own. —SELECTED

MARCH 21

All things work together for good to them that love God.
—Romans 8:28

If our circumstances find us in God, we will find God in all our circumstances. —SELECTED

MARCH 22

Their eyes were holden....Their eyes were opened.
—Luke 24:16, 31

There is much precious significance in this. The Lord is often present in our lives in things that we do not dream possess any significance. We are asking God about something that needs His mighty working, and the very instrument by which He is to work is by our side, perhaps for weeks and months and years all unrecognized, until suddenly, one day it grows luminous and glorious with the very presence of the Lord, and becomes the mighty instrument of His victorious working. He loves to show His hand through the unexpected. Often he keeps us from seeing His way until just before He opens it, and then, immediately as it is unfolded, we find that He was walking by our side in the very thing, long before we even suspected its meaning.   —A. B. SIMPSON

MARCH 23

But the path of the just is as the shining light, that shineth more and more unto the perfect day.
—Proverbs 4:18

Have I begun this path of heavenly love and knowledge now? Am I progressing in it? Do I feel some dawnings of the heavenly light, pledges and previews of the full day of glory? Let all God's dealings serve to quicken me in my way. Let every affection it may please Him to send, be as the moving pillar-cloud of old, beckoning me to move my tent onward, saying, *"Arise...and depart; for this is not your rest"* (Micah 2:10). Let me be often standing now on faith's lofty eminences, looking for "the day of the Lord," the rising sun that is to set no more in weeping clouds. Wondrous progression! How will all earth's learning, its boasted acquirements and eagle-eyed philosophy sink into the lispings of very infancy in comparison with this manhood of knowledge! Heaven will be the true "excelsior," its song, "a song of degrees," Jesus leading His people from height to height of glory, and saying, as He said to Nathaniel, "You will see greater things than these!" (John 1:50).   —MACDUFF

MARCH 24

They rest not day and night.
—Revelation 4:8

O blessed rest! When we rest not day and night, saying, *"Holy, holy, holy, Lord God Almighty!"* (Revelation 4:8). When we will rest from sin, but not from worship; from suffering and sorrow, but not from joy! O blessed day, when I will rest with God; when I will rest in knowing, loving, rejoicing, and praising; when my perfect soul and body will together perfectly enjoy the most perfect God, who is love itself, who will perfectly love me and rest in His love to me, and I will rest in my love to Him; when He will rejoice over me with joy, and joy over me with singing, and I will rejoice in Him! (See Zephaniah 3:17.)   —BAXTER

MARCH 25

*God saw the light, that it was good: and God divided
the light from the darkness.*
—Genesis 1:4

No sooner is there a good thing in the world
than a division is necessary. Light and darkness
have no communion. God has divided them; let us
not confound them. Sons of light must not have fellowship with deeds, doctrines, or deceits of darkness. The children of the day must be sober, honest,
and bold in their Lord's work, leaving the works of
darkness to those who will dwell in it forever. We
should divide the light from the darkness by our
distinct separation from the world. In judgment, in
action, in hearing, in teaching, and in association,
we must discern between the precious and the vile,
and maintain the great distinction that the Lord
made upon the world's first day.

O Lord Jesus, be our light throughout the whole
of this day, for Your light is the light of men.

—SPURGEON

MARCH 26

I have finished the work which thou gavest me to do.
—John 17:4

Was the work of the Master indeed done? Was
not its heaviest task yet to come? He had not yet
met the dread hour of death. Why did He say that

His work was done? It was because He knew that, when the will is given, the battle is ended. He was only in the shadows of the garden, but to conquer these shadows was already to conquer all. He who has willed to die has already triumphed over death. All that remains to Him is but the outer husk, the shell.

The cup that our Father gives us to drink is a cup for the will. It is easy for the lips to drain it when once the heart has accepted it. Not on the heights of Calvary, but in the shadows of Gethsemane is the cup presented. The act is easy after the choice. The real battlefield is in the silence of the spirit. Conquer there, and you are crowned.   —GEORGE MATHESON

MARCH 27

A great multitude...stood before the throne.
—Revelation 7:9

A station on the feet in front of the throne in heaven is the effect of being often on the knees before the throne on earth.   —SELECTED

MARCH 28

He that sent me is with me: the Father hath not left me alone; for I do always those things that please him.
—John 8:29

He who holds nearest communion with heaven is best able to discharge the duties of everyday life.
—SELECTED

MARCH 29

They that wait upon the Lord shall renew
their strength; they shall mount up with wings
as eagles; they shall run, and not be weary;
and they shall walk, and not faint.
—Isaiah 40:31

The eagle that soars in the upper air does not worry itself as to how it is to cross rivers.

—SELECTED

MARCH 30

She took for him an ark of bulrushes...and she laid it
in the flags by the river's brink.
—Exodus 2:3

The mother of Moses laid the ark in the flags by the river's brink. Aye, but before doing so, she laid it on the heart of God! She could not have laid it so courageously upon the Nile, if she had not first devoutly laid it upon the care and love of God.

We are often surprised at the outward calmness of men who are called upon to do unpleasant and most trying deeds; but if we could have seen them in secret, we would have known the moral preparation that they underwent before coming out to be seen by men. Be right in the sanctuary, if you would be right in the market place. Be steadfast in prayer, if you would be calm in affliction. Start your race from the throne of God itself, if you would run well, and win the prize.

—JOSEPH PARKER

MARCH 31

See then that ye walk circumspectly.
—Ephesians 5:15

There is no such thing as negative influence. We are all positive in the place we occupy, making the world better or making it worse.

—T. DEWITT TALMAGE

A P R I L

APRIL 1

In the morning came the word of the LORD unto me.
—Ezekiel 12:8

A quiet hour spent alone with God at the beginning of the day is the best beginning for the toils and cares of active business. A brief season of prayer, looking above for wisdom and grace and strength, and seeking for an outpouring of the Holy Spirit, helps us to carry our religion into the business of the day. It brings joy and peace within the heart. And as we place all our concerns in the care and keeping of the Lord, faithfully striving to do His will, we have a joyful trust that however dark or discouraging events may appear, our Father's hand is guiding everything, and will give the wisest direction to all our toils.   —AUTHOR UNKNOWN

APRIL 2

That night they caught nothing.
—John 21:3

God may let the sinful world succeed in their forbidden schemes, but, blessed be His name, He does not allow His chosen ones to prosper in the path that leads them out of His holy will! He has a storm to send after every Jonah, and an empty net for every unbelieving and inconsistent Simon.

—A. B. SIMPSON

APRIL 3

The LORD God formed man of the dust of the ground, and breathed into his nostrils the breath of life; and man became a living soul.
—Genesis 2:7

And so this soul of mine is a compound of two worlds—dust and Deity! It touches the boundary line of two hemispheres. It is allied on one side to the divine; on the other, to the beast of the field. Its beginning is from beneath, but its culmination is from above; it is started from the dust of the ground, but it is finished in the breath of God. My soul, are you living up to your twofold origin? Are you remembering your double parentage, and therefore your double duty? You have a duty to your God, for His breath is in you; you have a duty to the earth, for out of it were you taken.   —GEORGE MATHESON

APRIL

*All the land which thou seest, to thee will I give it, and
to thy seed for ever.*
—Genesis 13:15

God's promises are ever on the ascending scale. One leads up to another, fuller and more blessed than itself. In Mesopotamia God said, "I will show you the land." At Bethel, "This is the land." Here, "And I will give you all the land, and children innumerable as the grains of sand." We will find even these eclipsed.

It is thus that God allures us to saintliness. Not giving anything until we have dared to act—that He may test us. Not giving everything at first—that He may not overwhelm us. And always keeping in hand an infinite reserve of blessing. Oh, the unexplored remainders of God! Who ever saw His last star?   —F. B. MEYER

APRIL 5

*There stood by me this night the angel of God,...
saying, Fear not, Paul...God hath given thee all them
that sail with thee. Wherefore...be of good cheer: for I
believe God, that it shall be even as it was told me.*
—Acts 27:23–25

An active faith can give thanks for a promise, though it has not yet been performed; knowing that God's bonds are as good as ready money.
—MATTHEW HENRY

APRIL 6

They made me the keeper of the vineyards; but mine own vineyard have I not kept.
—Song of Solomon 1:6

Our attention is here drawn to a danger that is preeminently one of this day: the intense activity of our times may lead to zeal in service to the neglect of personal communion; but such neglect will not only lessen the value of the service, but tend to incapacitate us for the highest service.
—J. HUDSON TAYLOR

APRIL 7

We came unto the land whither thou sentest us....We saw the children of Anak there.
—Numbers 13:27–28

It is when we are in the way of duty that we find giants. It was when Israel was going forward that the giants appeared. When they turned back into the wilderness they found none.   —SELECTED

APRIL 8

Always rejoicing.
—2 Corinthians 6:10 ASV

No Christian can ever know what is meant by those two little words, *"always rejoicing,"* but the Christian who takes up his cross and follows Jesus.
—W. HAY AITKEN

APRIL 9

A daily rate for every day.
—2 Kings 25:30

One staff aids a traveler, but a bundle of staves is a heavy burden.   —SPURGEON

APRIL 10

Perfect love casteth out fear.
—1 John 4:18

Fear and love rise up in antagonism to each other as motives in life, like those two mountains from which respectively the blessings and curses of the old law were pronounced: the Mount of Cursing, all barren, stony, without verdure and without water; the Mount of Blessing, green and bright with many a flower, and blessed with many a trickling rill. Fear is barren. Love is fruitful. The one is a slave, and its work is little worth. The other is free, and its deeds are great and precious. From the summit of the mountain that genders to bondage may be heard the words of the law; but the power to keep all these laws must be sought on the sunny hill where liberty dwells in love and gives energy to obedience. Therefore, if you would use in your own life the highest power that God has given us for our growth in grace, draw your arguments, not from fear, but from love.

—ALEXANDER MACLAREN

APRIL 11

Each one resembled the children of a king.
—Judges 8:18

If the King is indeed near of kin to us, the royal likeness will be recognizable.
—FRANCES RIDLEY HAVERGAL

APRIL 12

He maketh me to lie down in green pastures: he leadeth me beside the still waters.
—Psalm 23:2

This suggests the rest into which our Good Shepherd leads His flock. Life is not all toil. God gives us many quiet resting places in our pilgrim way.

Night is one of these, when, after the day's toil, struggle, and exhaustion, we are led aside, the curtains are drawn to shut out the noise, and "He gives His beloved sleep" (Psalm 127:2), in sleep giving the wonderful blessings of renewal. The Sabbath is another of these quiet resting places. God would have us drop our worldly tasks and have a day for the refreshing of both body and soul. Friendship's trysts are also quiet resting places, where heart may commune with heart, where Jesus comes, too, unseen, and gives His blessing. All ordinances of Christian worship—seasons of prayer and devotion, hours of communion with God—are quiet resting places.

A P R I L

We need these silent times in our busy lives far more than we are apt to realize, needing them all the more the busier the life may be.   —J. R. MILLER

APRIL 13

Could ye not watch with me one hour?
—Matthew 26:40

Oh! ye who sigh and languish,
  And mourn your lack of power,
Heed ye this gentle whisper,
  "Could ye not watch one hour?"
To fruitfulness and blessing,
  There is no "royal road";
The power for holy service
  Is communion with God.
                    —AUTHOR UNKNOWN

APRIL 14

Work out your own salvation with fear and trembling.
For it is God which worketh in you both to will
and to do of his good pleasure.
—Philippians 2:12–13

It is not your business and mine to study whether we will get to heaven, or even to study whether we will be good men. It is our business to study how we will come into the midst of the purposes of God and have the unspeakable privilege in these few years of doing something of His work.
                    —PHILLIPS BROOKS

APRIL 15

*God...hath shined in our hearts, to give the light
of the knowledge of the glory of God
in the face of Jesus Christ.*
—2 Corinthians 4:6

Christian! Do not rest until you know the full, the unbroken shining of God in your heart. To this end, yield to every stirring of it that shows you some unconquered and perhaps unconquerable evil. Just bring it to the light; let the light shine upon it, and shine it out. Wait upon the Lord more than watchers for the morning, for *"the path of the just is as the shining light, that shineth more and more unto the perfect day"* (Proverbs 4:18). Count on it that God wants to fill you with the light of His glory: wait on Him more than watchers for the morning. *"Wait, I say, on the LORD"* (Psalm 27:14).

—ANDREW MURRAY

APRIL 16

*They that wait upon the LORD shall...mount up
with wings as eagles.*
—Isaiah 40:31

All creatures that have wings can escape from every snare that is set for them, if only they will fly high enough; and the soul that uses its wings can always find a sure "way to escape" from all that hurts or troubles it.　　　　—SMITH

APRIL

APRIL 17

*It is God which worketh in you both to will and
to do of his good pleasure.*
—Philippians 2:13

Full salvation is to realize that everything we see in Christ, our Example, may be ours, not by imitation, but by reproduction.   —SELECTED

APRIL 18

Consider how great things he hath done for you.
—1 Samuel 12:24

Look back on all the way the Lord your God has led you. Do you not see it dotted with ten thousand blessings in disguise? Call to mind the needed succor sent at the critical moment: the right way chosen for you, instead of the wrong way you had chosen for yourself; the hurtful thing to which your heart so fondly clung, removed out of your path; the breathing time granted, which your tired and struggling spirit just at the moment needed. Oh, has not Jesus stood at your side when you knew it not? Has not Infinite Love encircled every event with its everlasting arms, and gilded every cloud with its merciful lining? Oh, retrace your steps, and mark His footprint in each one! Thank Him for them all, and learn the needed lesson of leaning more simply on Jesus.

—F. WHITFIELD

APRIL 19

My soul, wait thou only upon God.
—Psalm 62:5

Did it ever occur to you that if you do not hear God's answer to prayer, it may be not because He is dumb, but because you are deaf; not because He has no answer to give, but because you have not been listening for it? We are so busy with our service, so busy with our work, and sometimes so busy with our praying, that it does not occur to us to stop our own talking and listen if God has some answer to give us with the *"still small voice"* (1 Kings 19:12); to be passive, to be quiet, to do nothing, say nothing, and, in some true sense, think nothing; simply to be receptive and waiting for the voice. *"Wait thou only upon God,"* said the psalmist; and again, *"Wait on the Lord"* (Psalm 27:14). —AUTHOR UNKNOWN

APRIL 20

*Bear ye one another's burdens, and so fulfil
the law of Christ.*
—Galatians 6:2

However perplexed you may at any hour become about some question of truth, one refuge and resource is always at hand: you can do something for someone besides yourself. At the times when you cannot see God, there is still open to you this sacred possibility: to show God. For it is the love

and kindness of human hearts through which the divine reality comes home to men, whether they name it or not. Let this thought, then, stay with you: there may be times when you cannot find help, but there is no time when you cannot give help.
—GEORGE MERRIAM

APRIL 21

Lo, I am with you all the days.
—Matthew 28:20 ASV

"All the days." In winter days, when joys are fled; in sunless days, when the clouds return again and again after rain; in days of sickness and pain; in days of temptation and perplexity, as much as in days when the heart is as full of joy as the woodlands in spring are full of song. That day never comes when the Lord Jesus is not at the side of His saints. Lover and friend may stand afar, but He walks with them through the fires; He fords with them the rivers; He stands by them when face to face with the lion. We can never be alone. We must always add His resources to our own when making our calculations. —F. B. MEYER

APRIL 22

My meat is to do the will of him that sent me.
—John 4:34

Seek your life's nourishment in your life's work.
—PHILLIPS BROOKS

APRIL 23

*I the L*ORD *thy God will hold thy right hand, saying*
unto thee, Fear not; I will help thee.
—Isaiah 41:13

Don't try to hold God's hand; let Him hold yours.
Let Him do the holding, and you do the trusting.
—H. W. WEBB-PEOPLE

APRIL 24

Be it unto thee even as thou wilt.
—Matthew 15:28

Oh, the victories of prayer! They are the mountaintops of the Bible. They take us back to the plains of Mamre, to the fords of Peniel, to the prison of Joseph, to the triumphs of Moses, to the transcendent victories of Joshua, to the deliverances of David, to the miracles of Elijah and Elisha, to the whole story of the Master's life, to the secret of Pentecost, to the keynote of Paul's unparalleled ministry, to the lives of saints and the deaths of martyrs, to all that is most sacred and sweet in the history of the church and the experience of the children of God. And when, for us, the last conflict has passed, and the footstool of prayer has given place to the harp of praise, the spots of time that will be gilded with the most celestial and eternal radiance will be those, often linked with deepest sorrow and darkest night, over which we have the inscription, "Jehovah-Shammah: the Lord was there!" —A. B. SIMPSON

APRIL 25

He...said,...I...hid thy talent in the earth...
His lord answered and said unto him,
Thou wicked and slothful servant.
—Matthew 25:24–26

Between the great things we cannot do and the small things we will not do, the danger is that we will do nothing. —MONOD

APRIL 26

Thou shalt know that I am the Lord: for they
shall not be ashamed that wait for me.
—Isaiah 49:23

Quiet waiting before God would save from many a mistake and from many a sorrow.

—J. HUDSON TAYLOR

APRIL 27

To him be glory both now and for ever.
—2 Peter 3:18

Believer, you are anticipating the time when you will join the saints above in ascribing all glory to Jesus, but are you glorifying Him now? The apostle's words are, *"To him be glory both now and for ever."* —SPURGEON

APRIL 28

*In every thing by prayer and supplication with
thanksgiving let your requests be made
known unto God.*
—Philippians 4:6

The natural temptation with every difficulty is to plan for it, to put it out of the way yourself; but stop short with all your planning, your thinking, your worry, and talk to Him! *"Cast thy burden upon the LORD, and he shall sustain thee"* (Psalm 55:22). You may not always be able to do this in a moment or two. Then keep on with your supplication until you know He has it, and prayer becomes praise. Rest, trust, and wait, and see how He does that which you wanted to do and had so much care about. *"Stand still, and see the salvation of the LORD"* (Exodus 14:13).   —A. E. FUNK

APRIL 29

The love of Christ constraineth us.
—2 Corinthians 5:14

The love of Christ is too large for any heart to hold it. It will overflow into others' hearts: it will give itself out, give itself away, for the enriching of other lives. The heart of Christ is a costly thing for anyone to have. It will lead those who have it where it led Him. If it cost Him the cross, it will cost them no less.   —J. M. CAMPBELL

APRIL

APRIL 30

*Having...boldness to enter into the holiest by the blood
of Jesus...let us draw near with a true heart.*
—Hebrews 10:19, 22

Oh, the glory of the message! For fifteen centuries Israel had a sanctuary with a Holiest of All, into which, under pain of death, no one might enter. Its one witness was that man cannot dwell in God's presence, cannot abide in His fellowship. And now how changed is all! As then the warning sounded, "No admittance! Enter not!" so now the call goes forth, "Enter in! The veil is rent; the Holiest is open; God waits to welcome you to His bosom; henceforth you are to live with Him." This is the message. Child, your Father longs for you to enter, to dwell, and to go out no more forever. —ANDREW MURRAY

M A Y

MAY 1

Thou art my God; early will I seek thee.
—Psalm 63:1

In a world where there is so much to ruffle the spirit's plumes, how needful is that entering into the secret of God's pavilion, which will alone bring it back to composure and peace! In a world where there is so much to sadden and depress, how blessed is the communion with Him in whom is the one true source and fountain of all true gladness and abiding joy! In a world where so much is ever seeking to unhallow our spirits, to render them common and profane, how high is the privilege of consecrating them anew in prayer to holiness and to God.   —ARCHBISHOP TRENCH

MAY 2

Be ye stedfast, unmoveable, always abounding in the work of the Lord.
—1 Corinthians 15:58

Activity in doing good is one recipe for being cheerful Christians; it is like exercise to the body, and it keeps the soul in health.   —BISHOP RYLE

MAY 3

In him was life; and the life was the light of men.
—John 1:4

Ye are the light of the world.
—Matthew 5:14

In the light we can walk and work. We walk in the light and become entirely children of light. We let our light, the light of God, shine, so that men may see our good works and glorify our Father in heaven. Gently, silently, lovingly, unceasingly, we give ourselves to transmit the light and the love God so unceasingly shines into us. Our one work is to wait, and admit, and then transmit the light of God in Christ.   —ANDREW MURRAY

MAY 4

Looking up to heaven, he sighed.
—Mark 7:34

Too often we sigh and look within; Jesus sighed and looked without. We sigh and look down; Jesus sighed and looked up. We sigh and look to earth; Jesus sighed and looked to heaven. We sigh and look to man; Jesus sighed and looked to God.

—STORK

MAY 5

His praise shall continually be in my mouth.
—Psalm 34:1

Do not let your praises be transient—a fit of music, and then the instrument hung by the wall until another gaudy day of some remarkable providence makes you take it down. God does not come as a guest to His saints' houses, but to dwell with them. David took this up for a life work: "As long as I live, I will praise you." (See Psalm 104:33.)

—GURNALL

MAY 6

Set your affection on things above,
not on things on the earth.
—Colossians 3:2

He who has his affections set on things above is like one who hangs on by the skies. And having a secure hold of these, he could say, though he saw the world roll away from beneath his feet, *"My heart is fixed, O God, my heart is fixed: I will sing and give praise"* (Psalm 57:7).　　—GUTHRIE

MAY 7

The blood of Jesus Christ his Son
cleanseth us from all sin.
—1 John 1:7

Learn a lesson from the eye of the miner, who all day long is working amid the flying coal dust. When he emerges in the light of day, his face may be grimy enough, but his eyes are clear and lustrous because the fountain of tears in the lachrymal gland is ever pouring its gentle tides over the eye, cleansing away each speck of dust as soon as it alights.

Is not this the miracle of cleansing that our spirits need in such a world as this? And this is what our blessed Lord is prepared to do for us by His cleansing blood, if only we will trust Him.

—F. B. MEYER

MAY 8

We glory in tribulations.
—Romans 5:3

Have you ever thought that someday you will never have anything to try you or anybody to vex you again?   —A. B. SIMPSON

MAY 9

The Lord is risen indeed, and hath appeared to Simon.
—Luke 24:34

MAY

Then...gladly received...[Peter's] word...and the
same day there were added unto them
about three thousand souls.
—Acts 2:41

Before the Lord can use us in His service we must have close individual dealings with Himself. He always will have to do in secret with that soul that which He intends to use in blessing others. Do you want to speak for Jesus to those around you? Then you must go to Jesus Himself for your message. What you say for Jesus must be gotten from Jesus. Oh, how much breath falls powerless on every side because it has not been inhaled in the sanctuary! We lack more secret dealing with the living God. We run without being sent: we speak before God has spoken to us. No wonder we so often fail. Oh, what secret prayer and what heart-searching discipline the heart needs before God can use it!   —F. WHITFIELD

MAY 10

Then said I, Woe is me! for I am undone; because I
am a man of unclean lips, and I dwell in the midst of
a people of unclean lips: for mine eyes have seen the
King, the LORD of hosts.
—Isaiah 6:5

It is not the sight of our sinful heart that humbles us; it is a sight of Jesus Christ. I am undone because my eyes have seen the King.
—ANDREW A. BONAR

MAY 11

The righteous eateth to the satisfying of his soul.
—Proverbs 13:25

Christ must satisfy; then, if we are not satisfied, it must be because we are not feeding on Him wholly and only. The fault is not in the provision that is made. —FRANCES RIDLEY HAVERGAL

MAY 12

Whom the Lord loveth he chasteneth.
—Hebrews 12:6

It has been well said that "earthly cares are a heavenly discipline," but they are even something better than discipline; they are God's chariots, sent to take the soul to its high places of triumph. In Song of Solomon we are told of *"a chariot...paved with love"* (Song of Solomon 3:9–10). We cannot always see the love lining to our own particular chariot—it often looks very unlovely—but every chariot sent by God must necessarily be paved with love, since God is love. It is His love indeed that sends the chariot.

Look upon your chastenings, then, no matter how grievous they may be for the present, as God's chariots, sent to carry your souls into the "high places" of spiritual achievement and uplifting, and you will find that they are, after all, *"paved with love."* —SMITH

MAY 13

*For this child I prayed; and the LORD hath given me
my petition which I asked of him: therefore also I
have lent him to the LORD; as long as he liveth
he shall be lent to the LORD.*
—1 Samuel 1:27–28

God sometimes bestows gifts just so that love may have something to renounce. The things that He puts into our hands are possibly put there that we may have the opportunity of showing what is in our heart. Oh, that there were in us a fervor of love that would lead us to examine everything that belongs to us, to ascertain how it might be made a means of showing our affection to Christ!   —GEORGE BOWEN

MAY 14

His kingdom ruleth over all.
—Psalm 103:19

"His kingdom ruleth over all." Therefore you can find nothing that is not matter for praise, since there is nothing that is not the matter of your Lord's gracious permission, planning, or control. *"Over all."* Nowhere can you step outside His realm, nor in anything get beyond His care and government. *"Over all."* Thus take all as from God, hold all as from God, and by your gratitude give all back to God again, completing the circle, making Him the Alpha and Omega, the Beginning and the End of all things.   —MARK GUY PEARSE

MAY 15

I know how to abound.
—Philippians 4:12

It is a dangerous thing to be prosperous. The crucible of adversity is a less severe trial to the Christian than the refining pot of prosperity. It needs more than human skill to carry the brimming cup of mortal joy with a steady hand, yet Paul had learned that skill, for he declared, *"In all things I am instructed both to be full and to be hungry"* (Philippians 4:12). When we have much of God's providential mercies, it often happens that we have but little of God's grace. Satisfied with earth, we are content to do without heaven. Rest assured, it is harder to know how to be full than it is to know how to be hungry, so desperate is the tendency of human nature to pride and forgetfulness of God. Take care that you ask in your prayers that God would teach you "how to be full."   —SPURGEON

MAY 16

Ye are the light of the world. A city that is set on an hill cannot be hid.
—Matthew 5:14

Lamps do not talk, but they do shine. A lighthouse sounds no drum; it beats no gong; and yet, far over the waters, its friendly spark is seen by the mariner. So let your actions shine out your religion.

Let the main sermon of your life be illustrated by all your conduct. —SPURGEON

MAY 17

Whosoever exalteth himself shall be abased; and he that humbleth himself shall be exalted.
—Luke 14:11

If you ask the way to the crown, 'tis by the cross; to the mountain, 'tis by the valley; to exaltation, 'tis he that humbles himself. —J. H. EVANS

MAY 18

For their sakes I sanctify myself, that they also might be sanctified through the truth.
—John 17:19

Do you remember, when Jesus was sitting with His disciples at the Last Supper, how He lifted up His voice and prayed, and in the midst of His prayer there came these wondrous words: *"For their sakes I sanctify myself, that they also might be sanctified"*? Is there anything in all the teachings that man has had from the lips of God that is nobler, that is more far-reaching than that—to be my best not simply for my own sake, but for the sake of the world? You can help your fellowmen. You must help your fellowmen; but the only way you can help them is by being the noblest and the best man that it is possible for you to be. —PHILLIPS BROOKS

MAY 19

Him they compelled to bear his cross.
—Matthew 27:32

There are many Christians of whom this is true. They are compelled to bear the cross, but how does it come? It comes by their running away from it. They make up their minds they won't have Christ's cross! And they find when the cross does come that it comes in a more terrible form, with a more crushing weight than ever it would have come had they only been content to submit themselves to the divine direction; for the cross has to come to all who are to be prepared for glory hereafter.

—W. HAY AITKEN

MAY 20

If we suffer, we shall also reign with him.
—2 Timothy 2:12

The highest bidder for the crown of glory is the lowliest wearer of the cross of self-denial.

—A. J. GORDON

MAY 21

Without me ye can do nothing.
—John 15:5

*I can do all things through Christ
which strengtheneth me.*
—Philippians 4:13

Apart from Him we can do nothing. While we are abiding in Him, nothing is impossible. The one purpose of our life should therefore be to remain in living and intense union with Christ, guarding against everything that would break it, employing every means of cementing and enlarging it. And just in proportion as we do so, we will find His strength flowing into us for every possible emergency. We may not feel its presence, but we will find it present whenever we begin to draw on it. There is no temptation that we cannot master, no privation that we cannot patiently bear, no difficulty with which we cannot cope, no work that we cannot perform, no confession or testimony that we cannot make, if only our souls are living in healthy union with Jesus Christ; for as our day or hour, so our strength will be. —F. B. MEYER

MAY 22

Whatsoever he saith unto you, do it.
—John 2:5

If I could give you information of my life, it would be to show how a woman of very ordinary ability has been led by God in strange and unaccustomed paths to do in His service what He has done in her. And if I could tell you all, you would see how God has done all, and I nothing. I have worked hard, very hard, that is all: and I have never refused God anything.
—FLORENCE NIGHTINGALE

MAY 23

He that is slow to anger is better than the mighty; and
he that ruleth his spirit than he that taketh a city.
—Proverbs 16:32

More dear than any other conquest in the sight of God and His angels is the conquest of self, which each man, with the help of heaven, can secure for himself.   —DEAN STANLEY

MAY 24

While I was musing the fire burned.
—Psalm 39:3

My soul, if you would muse more, the fire would burn more. Why do you not retire oftener with yourself? You would be better fitted for the world if you were less worldly. If you had more heavenly fire, you would have more earthly power.

Is there no secret pavilion into which you can go and warm yourself? Is there no holy of holies where you can catch a glow of impulse that will make you strong? Is it not written of the Son of Man that *"as he prayed, the fashion of his counte-nance was altered"* (Luke 9:29)? Yes, it was from His prayer that His tranfigured glory came. It was the glow of His heart that issued the glow of His countenance. It was when He was musing that the fire kindled.

MAY

O my soul, would you have your life glorified, beautified, transfigured to the eyes of men? Get up into the secret place of God's pavilion, where the fires of love are burning. Your life will shine gloriously to the dwellers on the plain. Your prayers will be luminous; they will light your face like the face of Moses when he did not know that it shone. Your words will be burning; they will kindle many a heart journeying on the road to Emmaus. Your path will be radiant; when you have prayed in Elijah's solitude, you will have Elijah's chariot of fire.

—GEORGE MATHESON

MAY 25

Whatsoever ye do,...do all in the name
of the Lord Jesus.
—Colossians 3:17

Do little things as if they were great, because of the majesty of the Lord Jesus Christ, who dwells in you; and do great things as if they were little and easy, because of His omnipotence.　　—PASCAL

MAY 26

Our Lord Jesus Christ...gave himself for our sins, that
he might deliver us from this present evil world.
—Galatians 1:3–4

Attachment to Christ is the only secret of detachment from the world.　　—A. J. GORDON

MAY 27

Hide thyself by the brook.
—1 Kings 17:3

Not by the river, but by the brook. The river would always contain an abundant supply, but the brook might dry up at any moment. What does this teach us? God does not place His people in luxuriance here. The world's abundance might withdraw their affections from Him. He does not give them the river, but the brook. The brook may be running today, tomorrow it may be dried up.

And why does God act thus? To teach us that we are not to rest in His gifts and blessings, but in Himself. This is what our hearts are always doing—resting in the gift, instead of the Giver. Therefore God cannot trust us by the river, for it unconsciously takes up His place in the heart. It is said of Israel that when they were full, they forgot God.   —F. WHITFIELD

MAY 28

Seek ye first the kingdom of God, and his
righteousness; and all these things shall
be added unto you.
—Matthew 6:33

We need have only one care, that we put the first thing first—faithfulness to God. Then all else we need for both worlds will be supplied. God will never fail us; but we forget, sometimes, in our rejoicing over such an assurance, that we must fulfill our part if we would claim the divine promise.

It will not always be easy. Tomorrow it may mean a distasteful task, a disagreeable duty, a costly sacrifice for one who does not seem worthy. Life is full of sore testings of our willingness to follow the Good Shepherd. We do not have the slightest right to claim this assurance unless we have taken Christ as the guide of our life. —J. R. MILLER

MAY 29

*Keep thy heart with all diligence; for out of it
are the issues of life.*
—Proverbs 4:23

He who would keep his heart pure and holy must plant a sentinel at every avenue by which sin may find access there, guarding against nothing more than the "little" sins, as they are called.

The man of God has his eyes to keep, and so Job said, *"I made a covenant with mine eyes"* (Job 31:1); his tongue, and hence the exhortation, *"Keep thy tongue from evil, and thy lips from speaking guile"* (Psalm 34:13); his ears, and hence the warning, *"Cease, my son, to hear the instruction that causeth to err"* (Proverbs 19:27); his feet, and hence David said, *"I have refrained my feet from every evil way, that I might keep thy word"* (Psalm 119:101). And since there is no gate of the five senses by which the enemy may not come in like a flood, unless the Spirit lifts up a standard against him, we have need to guard every port and write over every portal, "Here there enters nothing to hurt or to defile."

—GUTHRIE

MAY 30

I am not able to bear all this people alone,
because it is too heavy for me.
—Numbers 11:14

It is most needful for all servants of Christ to remember that whenever the Lord places a man in a position of responsibility, He will both fit him for it and maintain him in it. It is, of course, another thing altogether if a man will rush unsent into any field of work, or any post of difficulty or danger. In such a case, we may assuredly look for a thorough breakdown, sooner or later. But when God calls a man to a certain position, He will endow him with the needed grace to occupy it.

This holds good in every case. We can never fail if we only cling to the living God. We can never run dry if we are drawing from the fountain. Our tiny springs will soon dry up, but our Lord Jesus Christ declares, *"He that believeth on me, as the scripture hath said, out of his belly shall flow rivers of living water"* (John 7:38). —C. H. M.

MAY 31

Whosoever shall give to drink unto one of these
little ones a cup of cold water only in the name
of a disciple, verily I say unto you, he shall
in no wise lose his reward.
—Matthew 10:42

M A Y

We are in danger of looking too far for opportunities of doing good and communicating. In reaching for rhododendrons, we trample down the daisies. —SELECTED

J U N E

JUNE 1

As thy days, so shall thy strength be.
—Deuteronomy 33:25

I can do all things through Christ
which strengtheneth me.
—Philippians 4:13

He will not impose upon you one needless burden. He will not exact more than He knows your strength will bear. He will ask no Peter to come to Him on the water, unless He imparts at the same time strength and support on the unstable waves. He will not ask you to draw water if the well is too deep, or to withdraw the stone if too heavy. But neither at the same time will He admit as an impossibility that which, as a free and responsible agent, it is in your power to avert. He will not regard as your misfortune what is your crime.   —MACDUFF

....for sin and for uncleanness.
—Zechariah 13:1

You who have faith in the Fountain, frequent it. Beware of two errors that are very natural and very disastrous. Beware of thinking any sin too great for it, and beware of thinking any sin too small. There is not a sin so little that it may not be the germ of everlasting perdition; there is not a sin so enormous that a drop of atoning blood will not wash it away as utterly as if it were drowned in the depths of the sea.   —JAMES HAMILTON

JUNE 3

Well done, thou good and faithful servant....Thou
wicked and slothful servant.
—Matthew 25:21, 26

God holds us responsible not for what we have, but for what we might have; not for what we are, but for what we might be.   —MARK GUY PEARSE

JUNE 4

I am black...as the tents of Kedar.
—Song of Solomon 1:5

I am my beloved's, and his desire is toward me.
—Song of Solomon 7:10

JUNE

Nothing humbles the soul like sacred and intimate communion with the Lord, yet there is a sweet joy in feeling that He knows all, and, notwithstanding, loves us still.   —J. HUDSON TAYLOR

JUNE 5

*A certain man,...who never had walked...heard Paul
speak: who...perceiving that he had faith
to be healed, said...Stand upright on thy feet.
And he leaped and walked.*
—Acts 14:8–10

Where true faith is, it will induce obedience; and where it does induce obedience, it will always, in one form or another, bring a blessing.   —W. HAY AITKEN

JUNE 6

*Then said Martha unto Jesus, Lord,...I know, that...
whatsoever thou wilt ask of God, God will give it thee.
Jesus saith unto her, Thy brother shall rise again.
Martha saith unto him, I know that he shall rise again
in the resurrection at the last day.*
—John 11:21–24

Beware, in your prayer, above everything, of limiting God, not only by unbelief, but by fancying that you know what He can do. Expect unexpected things, above all that we ask or think. Each time you intercede, be quiet first and worship God in His glory. Think of what He can do, of how He delights to hear Christ, of your place in Christ. Then expect great things.   —ANDREW MURRAY

JUNE 7

Thou shalt never wash my feet.
—John 13:8

Whatever hinders us from receiving a blessing that God is willing to bestow upon us is not humility, but the mockery of it. A genuine humility will ever feel the need of the largest measures of grace, and will be perfected just in the degree in which that grace is bestowed. The truly humble man will seek to be filled with all the fullness of God, knowing that when so filled there is not the slightest place for pride or for self. —GEORGE BOWEN

JUNE 8

As many of you as have been baptized into Christ have put on Christ.
—Galatians 3:27

Not simply the righteousness of our Savior, not simply the beauty of His holiness or the graces of His character, are we to put on as a garment. The Lord Himself is our clothing. Every Christian is not only a Christ-bearer but a Christ-wearer. We are so to enter into Him by communion, to be so endued with His presence and embued with His Spirit that men shall see Him when they behold us, as they see our garments when they look upon our bodies.
—A. J. GORDON

JUNE 9

Let us not sleep, as do others.
—1 Thessalonians 5:6

There are many ways of promoting Christian wakefulness. Among them, let me strongly advise Christians to converse together concerning the ways of the Lord. Christian and Hopeful, as they journeyed toward the Celestial City, said to themselves: "To prevent drowsiness in this place, let us fall into good discourse."

Christians who isolate themselves and walk alone are very liable to grow drowsy. Hold Christian company, and you will be kept wakeful by it, and refreshed and encouraged to make quicker progress in the road to heaven.   —SPURGEON

JUNE 10

Cast thy burden upon the LORD,
and he shall sustain thee.
—Psalm 55:22

He that takes his own cares upon himself loads himself with an uneasy burden. The fear of what may come, expectation of what will come, desire of what will not come, and the inability to redress all these, must bring him continual torment.

I will cast my cares upon God. He has bid me to do so. They cannot hurt Him: He can redress them.
—HALL

JUNE 11

I know whom I have believed.
—2 Timothy 1:12

Personal acquaintance with Christ is a living thing. Like a tree that uses every hour for growth, it thrives in sunshine, it is refreshed by rain—even the storm drives it to fasten its grip more firmly in the earth for its support. So, troubled heart, in all experiences, say, "This comes that I may make closer acquaintance with my Lord."

—AUTHOR UNKNOWN

JUNE 12

Jesus constrained his disciples to get into a ship.
—Matthew 14:22

Jesus constrained them to go! One would think that if ever there was the certain promise of success in a mission, it was here. Surely, here, if anywhere, a triumphant issue might have been confidently predicted; and yet here, more than anywhere, there was seeming failure. He sent them out on a voyage, and they met a storm such as they had never yet experienced. Let me ponder this, for it has been so with me, too. I have sometimes felt myself impelled to act by an influence that seemed above me—constrained to put to sea. The belief that I was constrained gave me confidence, and I was sure of a calm voyage. But the result was outward failure.

The calm became a storm: the sea raged, the winds roared, the ship tossed in the midst of the waves, and my enterprise was wrecked before it could reach the land.

Was, then, my divine command a delusion? No, nor yet was my mission a failure. He did send me on that voyage, but He did not send me for my purpose. He had one end, and I had another. My end was the outward calm; His was my meeting with the storm. My end was to gain the harbor of a material rest; His was to teach me there is a rest even on the open sea. —GEORGE MATHESON

JUNE 13

Study to show thyself approved unto God,
a workman that needeth not to be ashamed,
rightly dividing the word of truth.
—2 Timothy 2:15

Have your tools ready; God will find you work.
—CHARLES KINGSLEY

JUNE 14

Thy heart is not right in the sight of God.
—Acts 8:21

The worst of all mockeries is a religion that leaves the heart unchanged: a religion that has everything but the love of Christ enshrined in the soul. —F. WHITFIELD

JUNE 15

Sleep on now, and take your rest.
—Mark 14:41

Never did that sacred opportunity to watch with Christ return to His disciples. Lost then, it was lost forever. And now when Jesus is still beholding the travail of His soul in the redemption of the world, if you fail to be with Him watching for souls as they that must give account, remember that the opportunity will never return. *"Watch ye therefore,"* says your Lord, *"lest coming suddenly he find you sleeping"* (Mark 13:35–36). —A. J. GORDON

JUNE 16

Come out from among them, and be ye separate.
—2 Corinthians 6:17

With all the world for His choice, God placed His ancient people in a very remarkable situation. On the north they were walled in by the snowy ranges of Lebanon; a barren desert formed their eastern boundary; far to the south stretched a sterile region, called the howling wilderness; while the sea—not then, as now, the highway of the nations, facilitating rather than impeding travel—lay on their west, breaking on a shore that had few harbors and no navigable rivers to invite the steps of commerce.

May we not find a great truth in the very position in which God placed His chosen people? It certainly teaches us that to be holy or sanctified, we must be a separate people—living in the world, but not of it—as oil, that may be mixed, but cannot be combined with water.   —GUTHRIE

JUNE 17

Be ye therefore perfect, even as your Father which is in heaven is perfect.
—Matthew 5:48

Seeking the aid of the Holy Spirit, let us aim at perfection. Let every day see some sin crucified, some battle fought, some good done, some victory won. Let every fall be followed by a rise, and every step gained become, not a resting place, but a new starting point for further and higher progress.
    —GUTHRIE

JUNE 18

Wait for the promise of the Father.
—Acts 1:4

When the day of Pentecost was fully come, they were all with one accord in one place....And they were all filled with the Holy Ghost.
—Acts 2:1, 4

Obedience to a divine prompting transforms it into a permanent acquisition.   —F. B. MEYER

JUNE 19

*For so hath the Lord commanded us, saying, I have
set thee to be a light of the Gentiles, that thou
shouldest be for salvation unto the ends of the earth.*
—Acts 13:47

*Ye shall be witnesses unto me...unto the uttermost
part of the earth.*
—Acts 1:8

Men are questioning now, as they never have questioned before, whether Christianity is indeed the true religion that is to be the salvation of the world. Christian men, it is for us to give our bit of answer to that question. It is for us, in whom the Christian church is at the moment partially embodied, to declare that Christianity, that the Christian faith, the Christian manhood can do for the world what the world needs.

You ask, "What can I do?" You can furnish one Christian life. You can furnish a life so faithful to every duty, so ready for every service, so determined not to commit sin, that the great Christian church will be the stronger for your living in it, and the problem of the world be answered, and a certain great peace come into this poor, perplexed phase of our humanity as it sees that new revelation of what Christianity is.   —PHILLIPS BROOKS

JUNE 20

Endure...as a good soldier of Jesus Christ.
—2 Timothy 2:3

Life is not victory, but battle. Be patient a little longer. By and by, each in his turn, we will hear the sunset gun. —SELECTED

JUNE 21

As my Father hath sent me, even so send I you.
—John 20:21

We should never leave our room until we have seen the face of our dear Master, Christ, and have realized that we are being sent forth by Him to do His will and to finish the work that He has given us to do. He who said to His immediate followers, *"As my Father hath sent me, even so send I you,"* says as much to each one of us, as the dawn summons us to live another day. We should realize that we are as much sent forth by Him as the angels who *"do his commandments, hearkening unto the voice of his word"* (Psalm 103:20). There is some plan for each day's work, which He will unfold to us, if only we will look up to Him to do so; some mission to fulfill; some ministry to perform; some lesson patiently to learn, that we may be able to reach others also. As to our plans, we need not be anxious, because He who sends us forth is responsible to make the plan, according to His infinite wisdom, and to reveal it to us, however dull and stupid our faculties are. As to our sufficiency, we are secure in having all needed grace, because He never sends us forth, except He first breathes on us and says, *"Receive ye the Holy Ghost"* (John 20:22). There is always a special endowment for special power. —F. B. MEYER

JUNE 22

We have known and believed the love
that God hath to us.
—1 John 4:16

The secret of walking closely with Christ, and working successfully for Him, is to fully realize that we are His beloved. Let us but feel that He has set His heart upon us; that He is watching us from those heavens with tender interest; that He is working out the mystery of our lives with solicitude and fondness; that He is following us day by day as a mother follows her babe in his first attempt to walk alone; that He has set His love upon us and, in spite of us, is working out for us His highest will and blessing, as far as we will let Him. Then nothing can discourage us. Our hearts will glow with responsive love. Our faith will spring to meet His mighty promises, and our sacrifices will become the very luxuries of love for one so dear. This was the secret of John's spirit. *"We have known and believed the love that God hath to us."* And the heart that has fully learned this has found the secret of unbounded faith and enthusiastic service.

—A. B. SIMPSON

JUNE 23

Whosoever doth not bear his cross, and come after
me, cannot be my disciple.
—Luke 14:27

There is always the shadow of the cross resting upon the Christian's path. Is that a reason why you should avoid or not undertake the duty? Have you made up your mind that you will follow your Master everywhere else, save when He ascends the path that leads to the cross? Is that your religion? The sooner you change it, the better. The religion of the Lord Jesus Christ is the religion of the cross, and unless we take up our cross, we can never follow Him. —W. HAY AITKEN

JUNE 24

The Holy Ghost said, Separate me Barnabas and Saul
for the work whereunto I have called them.
—Acts 13:2

We have such a nice little quiet shady corner in the vineyard, down among the tender grapes, with such easy little weedings and waterings to attend to. And then the Master comes and draws us out into the thick of the work, puts us in a part of the field where we never would have thought of going, and puts larger tools into our hands, that we may do more at a stroke. And we know we are not sufficient for these things, and the very tools seem too heavy for us, and the glare too dazzling and the vines too tall. Ah, but would we dally, go back? He would not be in the shady corner with us now, for when He put us forth, He went before us. And it is only by close following that we can abide with Him.
—FRANCES RIDLEY HAVERGAL

JUNE 25

What I do thou knowest not now;
but thou shalt know hereafter.
—John 13:7

God keeps a school for His children here on earth, and one of His best teachers is disappointment. My friend, when you and I reach our Father's house, we will look back and see that the sharp-voiced, rough-visaged teacher Disappointment was one of the best guides to train us for it. He gave us hard lessons; he often used the rod; he often led us into thorny paths; he sometimes stripped off a load of luxuries; but that only made us travel the freer and the faster on our heavenward way. He sometimes led us down into the valley of the death-shadow; but never did the promises read so sweetly as when spelled out by the eye of faith in that very valley. Nowhere did he lead us so often, or teach us such sacred lessons, as at the cross of Christ. Dear, old, rough-handed teacher! We will build a monument to you yet, and crown it with garlands, and inscribe on it: Blessed be the memory of disappointment!   —THEODORE CUYLER

JUNE 26

These...have turned the world upside down.
—Acts 17:6

The serene beauty of a holy life is the most powerful influence in the world next to the might of God.   —PASCAL

JUNE 27

I am with thee, and will keep thee in all places whither thou goest, and will bring thee again into this land.
—Genesis 28:15

"With you," companionship; "keep you," guardianship; "bring you," guidance.   —SELECTED

JUNE 28

Be perfect, be of good comfort.
—2 Corinthians 13:11

A glance at the words is enough to make us feel how contradictory they are. *"Be perfect"*: that is a phrase that strikes us with despair. At once we feel how far away we are from our own poor ideal, and, alas, how much further from God's ideal concerning us. *"Be of good comfort"*: ah, that is very different! That seems to say, "Do not fret; do not fear. If you are not what you would be, you must be thankful for what you are."

Now the question is this: how can these two be reconciled? It is only the religion of Jesus Christ that reconciles them. He stands in our midst, and with the right hand of His righteousness He points us upward and says, *"Be perfect."* There is no resting place short of that. Yet with the left hand of His love He does encompass us, as He says, "Soul, be of good comfort; for that is what I came to do for you."
—MARK GUY PEARSE

JUNE 29

Small things.
—Zechariah 4:10

It is the little words you speak, the little thoughts you think, the little things you do or leave undone, the little moments you waste or use wisely, the little temptations that you yield to or overcome— the little things of every day that are making or marring your future life.   —SELECTED

JUNE 30

David inquired of the LORD.
—2 Samuel 5:19

Christian, if you would know the path of duty, take God for your compass; if you would steer your ship through dark billows, put the tiller in the hand of the Almighty. Many rocks might be escaped if we let our Father take the helm; we might well avoid many shoals or quicksands if we leave it to His sovereign will to choose and to command. The Puritan said, "As sure as ever a Christian carves for himself, he'll cut his own fingers." *"I will instruct thee and teach thee in the way which thou shalt go"* (Psalm 32:8) is God's promise to His people. Let us, then, take all our perplexities to Him and say, "Lord, what will You have me to do?" Do not leave your chamber this morning without inquiring of the Lord.   —SPURGEON

J U L Y

JULY 1

He laid his right hand upon me,
saying unto me, Fear not.
—Revelation 1:17

One of Wellington's officers, when commanded to go on some perilous duty, lingered a moment as if afraid, and then said, "Let me have one clasp of your all-conquering hand before I go; and then I can do it."

Seek the clasp of Christ's hand before every bit of work, every hard task, every battle, every good deed. Bend your head in the dewy freshness of the morning, before you go forth to meet the day's duties and perils, and wait for the benediction of Christ, as He lays His hands upon you. They are hands of blessing. Their touch will inspire you for courage, strength, and all beautiful and noble living.

—J. R. MILLER

JULY 2

Do thou that which is good.
—2 Kings 10:5

Keep as few good intentions hovering about as possible. They are like ghosts haunting a dwelling. The way to lay them is to find bodies for them. When they are embodied in substantial deeds they are no longer dangerous.   —WILLIAM ARNOT

JULY 3

Isaac dwelt by the well Lahairoi.
—Genesis 25:11

Isaac dwelt there, and made the well of the living and all-seeing God his constant source of supply. The usual tenor of a man's life, the dwelling of his soul, is the true test of his state. Let us learn to live in the presence of the living God. Let us pray to the Holy Spirit that this day, and every other day, we may feel, "You, God, see me." May the Lord Jehovah be as a well to us, delightful, comforting, unfailing, springing up into eternal life. The bottle of the creature cracks and dries up, but the well of the Creator never fails. Happy is he who dwells at the well, and so has abundant and constant supplies near at hand!

Glorious Lord, constrain us that we may never leave You, but dwell by the well of the living God!
—SPURGEON

JULY

JULY 4

Being seen of them forty days, and speaking of the things pertaining to the kingdom of God.
—Acts 1:3

This lingering for forty days is the crowning proof of Christ's tender regard for His little flock. He who had laid down His life for them is loath to leave them. Though they had forsaken Him and doubted Him, they had not wearied, much less had they worn out, His love. He stays to look again, and yet again, and yet again, upon them, as if turning back and lingering to bless them. It is consistent with His life of love. Everywhere He meets them without a touch of condemnation, without recalling a single memory of all His bitter suffering, revealing Himself to the disciples with a tenderness and blessedness indescribably beautiful.

How can He go until He has healed the Magdalene's broken heart? He must linger until poor Peter can venture near to have his forgiveness assured. He must stay to strengthen Thomas' faith. He must tarry with them until He has made them feel that He is just the same friendly, brotherly Jesus that He has ever been, caring for them in their work, watching them with a yearning pity, stooping to kindle a fire for their warmth, and to cook the fish for their meal, and then to bid them come and dine.

—MARK GUY PEARSE

JULY 5

Jesus,...being wearied with his journey, sat thus on the well....(For his disciples were gone away unto the city to buy meat.)...And many of the Samaritans of that city believed on him for the saying of the woman, which testified, He told me all that ever I did.
—John 4:6, 8, 39

The bits of wayside work are very sweet. Perhaps the odd bits, when all is done, will really come to more than the seemingly greater pieces! It is nice to know that the King's servants are always really on duty, even while some can only stand and wait.
—FRANCES RIDLEY HAVERGAL

JULY 6

He [John] saith, Behold the Lamb of God! And the two disciples heard him speak, and they followed Jesus.
—John 1:36–37

To be a Christian means to know the presence of a true personal Christ among us, and to follow.
—PHILLIPS BROOKS

JULY 7

Judas Iscariot...was a thief, and had the bag, and bare what was put therein.
—John 12:4, 6

Freely ye have received, freely give.
—Matthew 10:8

Ah, but if we should go thoroughly into this matter, would we not probably find that many of us are guilty, in some modified and yet sufficiently alarming sense, of treachery to the poor? Are we not, some of us, sent to them with benefactions that never reach them, and are only unconscious of guilt because we are so long accustomed to look upon the goods as bestowed on us, whereas the light of God's Word would plainly reveal upon those goods the names of the poor and needy?

—GEORGE BOWEN

JULY 8

Let every man take heed how he buildeth.
—1 Corinthians 3:10

Our business is not to build quickly, but to build upon a right foundation, and in a right spirit. Life is more than a mere competition as between man and man; it is not who can be done first, but who can work best; it is not who can rise highest in the shortest time, but who is working most patiently and lovingly in accordance with the designs of God.

—JOSEPH PARKER

JULY 9

As thy days, so shall thy strength be.
—Deuteronomy 33:25

No day without its duty; no duty without strength to perform it.   —SELECTED

JULY 10

Behold the man!
—John 19:5

"Behold the man!" was Pilate's jeer. That is what all the ages have been doing since, and the vision has grown more and more glorious. As they have looked, the crown of thorns has become a crown of golden radiance, and the cast-off robe has glistened like the garments He wore on the night of the Transfiguration. Martyrs have smiled in the flames at that vision. Sinners have turned at it to a new life. Little children have seen it, and have had awakened by it dim recollections of their heaven home. Toward it the souls of men yearn ever.

—ROBERT E. SPEER

JULY 11

Surely the LORD is in this place; and I knew it not.
—Genesis 28:16

"Surely the Lord was in this place; and I knew it not." My soul, this is also your experience! How often have you said in your sorrow, "Truly you are a God that hides Yourself!" How often have you slept with extreme heaviness of heart and desired not to wake again? But when you did wake again, the darkness was all a dream! Your vision of yesterday was a delusion. God had been with you all the night with that radiance that has no need of the sun.

O my soul, it is not only after the future you must aspire; you must aspire to see the glory of your past. You must find the glory of that way by which your God has led you, and be able even of your sorrow to say, "This was the gate of heaven!"
—GEORGE MATHESON

JULY 12

Awake, O north wind; and come, thou south; blow upon my garden, that the spices thereof may flow out.
—Song of Solomon 4:16

There are two winds mentioned in this beautiful prayer. God may send either or both as seems good to Him. He may send the north wind of conviction, to bring us to repentance, or He may send the south wind of love, to melt us into gratitude and holy joy. If we often require the sharp blasts of trial to develop our graces, do we not also need the warm south breezes of His mercy? Do we not need the new sense of Christ's presence in our hearts and the joys of the Holy Ghost? Do we not need to be melted, yes, to be overpowered by the love of Jesus? —THEODORE CUYLER

JULY 13

My meat is to do the will of him that sent me.
—John 4:34

The real secret of an unsatisfied life lies too often in an unsurrendered will. —J. HUDSON TAYLOR

JULY 14

*The mother of Jesus saith unto him, They have no
wine. Jesus saith unto her, Woman, what have
I to do with thee? mine hour is not yet come.
His mother saith unto the servants, Whatsoever
he saith unto you, do it.*
—John 2:3–5

In asking for temporal blessings, true wisdom lies in putting the matter into the Lord's hand and leaving it there. He knows our sorrows, and, if He sees it is good for us that the water would be turned into wine, He will do it. It is not for us to dictate; He sees what is best for us. When we ask for prosperity, perhaps the thing that we should have is trial. When we want to be relieved of a *"thorn in the flesh"* (2 Corinthians 12:7), He knows what we should have is an apprehension of the fact that His grace is sufficient for us. So we are put into His school and have to learn the lessons He has to teach us.   —W. HAY AITKEN

JULY 15

Ye shall not eat of it.
—Genesis 3:3

The sin of Paradise was eating the Tree of Knowledge before the Tree of Life. Life must ever be first. Knowing and not being, hearing and not doing, admiring and not possessing, all are light without life.   —SELECTED

JULY 16

*Let patience have her perfect work, that ye may be
perfect and entire, wanting nothing.*
—James 1:4

Are you where God would have you be? If not, come out, and at once, for you certainly ought not to be there. If you are, then be afraid to complain of circumstances that God has ordained on purpose to work out in you the very image and likeness of His Son. —MARK GUY PEARSE

JULY 17

*Sin, taking occasion by the commandment,
deceived me, and by it slew me.*
—Romans 7:11

Christian, beware how you think lightly of sin. Take heed lest you fall little by little. Sin, a little thing? Is it not a poison? Who knows its deadliness? Sin, a little thing? Do not the little foxes spoil the grapes? Does not the tiny coral insect build a rock that wrecks a navy? Do not little strokes fell lofty oaks? Will not continual droppings wear away stones? Sin, a little thing? It girded the Redeemer's head with thorns and pierced His heart! It made Him suffer anguish, bitterness, and woe. Could you but weigh the least sin in the scales of eternity, you would fly from it as from a serpent and abhor the least appearance of evil. Look upon all sin as that which crucified the Savior, and you will see it to be *"exceeding sinful"* (Romans 7:13). —SPURGEON

117

JULY 18

Awake, O north wind; and come, thou south; blow upon my garden, that the spices thereof may flow out.
—Song of Solomon 4:16

Sometimes God sends severe blasts of trial upon His children to develop their graces. Just as torches burn most brightly when swung violently to and fro, just as the juniper plant smells sweetest when flung into the flames, so the richest qualities of a Christian often come out under the north wind of suffering and adversity. Bruised hearts often emit the fragrance that God loves to smell. Almost every true believer's experience contains the record of trials which were sent for the purpose of shaking the spice tree.   —THEODORE CUYLER

JULY 19

Lord, my servant lieth at home sick of the palsy.
—Matthew 8:6

We, in this age of the church, are in the position of that sick servant at Capernaum. To the eye of sense, we are separated from the Savior. We do not see Him; we cannot touch Him; the hand cannot steal amid the crowd to catch His garment hem; we cannot hear His loved footsteps as of old on our threshold. But faith penetrates the invisible; the messenger, prayer, meets Him in the streets of the New Jerusalem; and faith and prayer together, the twin delegates from His church below, He has never yet sent away empty. —MACDUFF

JULY 20

Hold thou me up, and I shall be safe.
—Psalm 119:117

Do not spoil the chime of this morning's bells by ringing one-half a peal! Do not say, "Hold me up," and stop there, or add, "But all the same I will stumble and fall!" Finish the peal with God's own music, the bright words of faith that He puts into your mouth: "Hold me up, and I shall be safe!"
—FRANCES RIDLEY HAVERGAL

JULY 21

Sow beside all waters.
—Isaiah 32:20

Never mind where your work is. Never mind whether it is visible or not. Never mind whether your name is associated with it. You may never see the issues of your toils. You are working for eternity. If you cannot see results here in the hot working day, the cool evening hours are drawing near, when you may rest from your labors, and then they will follow you. So do your duty, and trust God to give the seed you sow *"a body as it hath pleased Him."* —ALEXANDER MACLAREN

JULY 22

Sinners; of whom I am chief....Now unto the King eternal, immortal, invisible, the only wise God, be honour and glory for ever and ever. Amen.
—1 Timothy 1:15, 17

Only those who have struck the deepest note of penitence can reach the highest note of praise.
—A. J. GORDON

JULY 23

Work out your own salvation with fear and trembling. For it is God which worketh in you both to will and to do of his good pleasure.
—Philippians 2:12–13

What a staggering weight of thought is excited by these words! Stay, my soul, and wonder that the Eternal God would stoop to work within your narrow limits. Is it not a marvel indeed, that He, whom the heavens cannot contain, and in whose sight they are not clean, would trouble Himself to work on such material, so unpromising, and amid circumstances so uncongenial? How careful should we be to make Him welcome and to throw no hindrance in His way! How eager to garner up all the least movements of His gracious operation, as the machinist conserves the force of his engine, and as the goldsmith, with miserly care, collects every flake of goldleaf! Surely we will be sensible of the fear of holy reverence and the trembling of eager anxiety, as we *"work out,"* into daily act and life, all that God our Father is "working in." —F. B. MEYER

JULY 24

Grow in grace, and in the knowledge of our Lord and Saviour Jesus Christ.
—2 Peter 3:18

Grace has its dawn as well as day; grace has its green blade, and afterwards its ripe corn in the ear; grace has its babes and its men in Christ. With God's work there, as with all His works, *"in all places of his dominion"* (Psalm 103:22), progress is both the prelude and the path to perfection. Therefore we are exhorted to *"grow in grace, and in the knowledge of our Lord and Saviour Jesus Christ,"* to go on to perfection, saying with Paul, *"I count not myself to have apprehended: but this one thing I do, forgetting those things which are behind, and reaching forth unto those things which are before, I press toward the mark for the prize of the high calling of God in Christ Jesus"* (Philippians 3:13–14).   —GUTHRIE

JULY 25

Let him that thinketh he standeth take heed lest he fall.
—1 Corinthians 10:12

Angels fell in heaven, Adam in paradise, Peter in Christ's presence.   —THEOPHILUS POLWHEILE

JULY 26

Giving all diligence, add to your faith virtue.
—2 Peter 1:5

You will find it less easy to unroot faults than to choke them by gaining virtues. Do not think of your faults, still less of others' faults; in every person who comes near you, look for what is good and strong; honor that; rejoice in it, and, as you can, try to imitate it; and your faults will drop off, like dead leaves, when their time comes.

—JOHN RUSKIN

JULY 27

Peace I leave with you, my peace I give unto you....Let not your heart be troubled, neither let it be afraid.
—John 14:27

Dark hours come to us all; and if we have no clue to a peace that can pass unbroken through their murky gloom, we will be in a state of continual dread. Any stone flung by a chance passerby may break the crystal clearness of the lake of peace and send disturbing ripples across it, unless we have learned to trust in the perpetual presence of Him who can make and keep a "great calm" within the soul. Only let nothing come to you that you will not instantly hand over to Him—all petty worries, all crushing difficulties, all inability to believe.

—F. B. MEYER

JULY 28

Your heavenly Father knoweth.
—Matthew 6:32

The master judges by the result, but our Father judges by the effort. Failure does not always mean fault. He knows how much things cost and weighs them where others only measure. Your Father! Think how great a store His love sets by the poor beginnings of the little ones, clumsy and unmeaning as they may be to others. All this lies in this blessed relationship, and infinitely more. Do not fear to take it all as your own. —MARK GUY PEARSE

JULY 29

Cleanse thou me from secret faults.
—Psalm 19:12

The world wants men who are saved from secret faults. The world can put on an outside goodness and go very far in uprightness and morality, and it expects that a Christian will go beyond it and be free from secret faults. A little crack will spoil the ring of the coin. The world expects, and rightly, that the Christian should be more gentle and patient and generous than he who does not profess to be a disciple of the Lord Jesus. For the sake of those who take their notion of religion from our lives, we need to put up this prayer earnestly, "Cleanse me from secret faults." —MARK GUY PEARSE

JULY 30

Ye are dead, and your life is hid with Christ in God.
—Colossians 3:3

It is neither talent, nor power, nor gifts that do the work of God, but it is that which lies within the power of the humblest; it is the simple, earnest life hidden with Christ in God.   —F. W. ROBERTSON

JULY 31

Blessed is the man...that keepeth the sabbath.
—Isaiah 56:2

The Sabbath is the savings bank of human life, into which we deposit one day in seven to be repaid in the autumn of our life with compound interest.
—SELECTED

A U G U S T

AUGUST 1

Continue in prayer.
—Colossians 4:2

The greatest and the best talent that God gives to any man or woman in this world is the talent of prayer. And the best usury that any man or woman brings back to God when He comes to reckon with him or her at the end of this world is a life of prayer. And those servants best put their Lord's money to the exchangers who rise early and sit late, as long as they are in this world, ever finding out, and ever following after better and better methods of prayer, and ever forming more secret, more steadfast, and more spiritually fruitful habits of prayer, until they literally pray without ceasing, and until they continually strike out into new enterprises in prayer and new achievements and new enrichments.

—ALEXANDER WHYTE

AUGUST 2

They took knowledge of them,
that they had been with Jesus.
—Acts 4:13

If I think of the world, I get the impress of the world; if I think of my trials and sorrows, I get the impress of my trials and sorrows; if I think of my failures, I get the impress of my failures; if I think of Christ, I get the impress of Christ.   —SELECTED

AUGUST 3

The word of God, which liveth and abideth for ever.
—1 Peter 1:23

The Word abides. The Jew hated it, but it lived on, while the veil was torn away from the shrine that the Shekinah had forsaken and while Jerusalem itself was destroyed. The Greek derided it, but it has seen his philosophy barren and his Acropolis in ruins. The Romans threw it into the flames, but it rose from its ashes and swooped down upon the falling eagle. The reasoner cast it into the furnace, which his own negligence had heated "seven times more than was customary" (see Daniel 3:19), but it came out without the smell of fire. The formalist fastened serpents around it to poison it, but it shook them off and felt no harm. The infidel cast it overboard in a tempest of sarcasm, but it rode gallantly upon the crest of the proud waters. And it is living still, yet heard in the loudest swelling of the storm. It has been speaking all the while; it is speaking now! —PUNSHON

AUGUST 4

Now are ye light in the Lord: walk as children of light.
—Ephesians 5:8

We do not realize the importance of the unconscious part of our life ministry. It goes on continually. In every greeting we give to another, in every moment's conversation, in every letter we write, in every contact with other lives, there is a subtle influence that goes from us that reaches further, and leaves a deeper impression, than the things themselves that we are doing. It is not so much what we do as what we are, that tells in spiritual results and impressions. —J. R. MILLER

AUGUST 5

As for thee, the Lord thy God hath not suffered thee so to do.
—Deuteronomy 18:14

What a stepping stone! We give thanks, often with a tearful, doubtful voice, for our spiritual mercies positive, but what an almost infinite field there is for mercies negative! We cannot even imagine all that our God has suffered us not to do, not to be.
—FRANCES RIDLEY HAVERGAL

AUGUST 6

He entered into one of the ships...and...sat down.
—Luke 5:3

When Jesus sits in the ship, everything is in its right place. The cargo is in the hold, not in the heart. Cares and gains, fears and losses, yesterday's failure and today's success do not thrust themselves in between us and His presence. The heart clings to Him. *"Goodness and mercy shall follow me"* (Psalm 23:6), sang the psalmist. Alas, when the goodness and mercy come before us, and our blessings shut Jesus from view! Here is the blessed order: the Lord ever first, I following Him, His goodness and mercy following me.

—MARK GUY PEARSE

AUGUST 7

Let us lay aside every weight, and the sin which doth so easily beset us, and let us run with patience the race that is set before us, looking unto Jesus.
—Hebrews 12:1–2

Think, as you sit here, of anything that you are doing that is wrong, of any habit of your life, of your self-indulgence, or of that great, pervasive habit of your life that makes you a creature of the present instead of the eternities, a creature of the material earth instead of the glorious skies. Ask yourself of any habit that belongs to your own

personal life, and bring it face to face with Jesus
Christ. —PHILLIPS BROOKS

AUGUST 8

*Set your affection on things above,
not on things on the earth.*
—Colossians 3:2

*Whatsoever thy hand findeth to do,
do it with thy might.*
—Ecclesiastes 9:10

If we are to live separate from the world, how,
since men only do well what they do with a will,
are we, with affections fixed on things above,
to perform aright the secular, ordinary duties of
life? If our hearts are engrossed with heavenly
things, how are we to obey this other and equally
divine commandment, "Whatsoever your hand
finds to do, do it with your might"? The two
are perfectly consistent. Standing between the
celestial and terrestrial worlds, man is related
to both. Resembling neither a flower, which,
springing from the dust and returning to it,
belongs altogether to the earth, nor a star, which,
shining far remote from its lower sphere, belongs
altogether to the heavens, our hearts may be
compared to the rainbow, which, rising into
heaven but resting on earth, is connected both
with the clods of the valley and the clouds of the
sky. —GUTHRIE

AUGUST 9

He...began to wash the disciples' feet.
—John 13:5

We forget that Jesus Christ is the same today, when He is sitting on the throne, as He was yesterday, when He trod the pathway of our world. In this forgetfulness how much we miss! What He was, that He is. What He said, that He says. The Gospels are simply specimens of the life that He is ever living; they are leaves torn out of the diary of His unchangeable Being. Today He is engaged in washing the feet of His disciples, soiled with their wilderness journeyings. Yes, that charming incident is having its fulfillment in you, my friend, if only you do not refuse the lowly loving offices of Him whom we call Master and Lord, but who still girds Himself and comes forth to serve. And we must have this incessant cleansing if we would keep right. It is not enough to look back to an hour when we first knelt at the feet of the Son of God for pardon and heard Him say, "Your sins, which are many, are all forgiven" (Luke 7:47). We need daily, hourly cleansing from daily, hourly sin. —F. B. MEYER

AUGUST 10

The Father sent the Son to be the Saviour of the world.
—1 John 4:14

It is a sweet thought that Jesus Christ did not come forth without His Father's permission, authority, consent, and assistance. He was sent of the Father that He might be the Savior of men. Did you ever consider the depth of love in the heart of Jehovah, when God the Father equipped His Son for the great enterprise of mercy? If not, be this your day's meditation. The Father sent Him! Contemplate that subject. Think how Jesus works what the Father wills. In the wounds of the dying Savior, see the love of the great I AM. Let every thought of Jesus be also connected with the eternal, ever-blessed God. —SPURGEON

AUGUST 11

They that wait upon the LORD shall
renew their strength.
—Isaiah 40:31

Lord, what a change within us one short hour
Spent in Thy presence will prevail to make!
What heavy burdens from our bosoms take!
What parched grounds refresh us with a shower!
We kneel—and all around us seems to lower.
We rise—and all the distant and the near
Stand forth in sunny outline, brave and clear.
We kneel—how weak: we rise—how full of power.
Why, therefore, should we do ourselves this wrong
Or others—that we are not always strong;
That we are ever overborne with care;
That we should ever weak or heartless be,
Anxious or troubled, while with us is prayer,
And joy and strength and courage are with Thee?
—ARCHBISHOP TRENCH

AUGUST 12

Go in this thy might...have not I sent thee?
—Judges 6:14

God never leaves His child to fail when in the path of obedience. —THEODORE CUYLER

AUGUST 13

Created in Christ Jesus unto good works.
—Ephesians 2:10

Let us ask Him to work in us to will those good works, so that our wills, without being impaired in their free operation, may be permeated and molded by His will, just as light suffuses the atmosphere without displacing it. And let us also expect that He will infuse into us sufficient strength that we may be able to do His will unto all pleasing. Thus, day by day, our lives will be a manifestation of those holy volitions and lovely deeds that will attest to the indwelling and inworking of God. And men will see our good works, and glorify our Father who is in heaven. —F. B. MEYER

AUGUST 14

Thou shalt have no other gods before me.
—Exodus 20:3

If you find yourself beginning to love any plea-sure better than your prayers, any book better than your Bible, any house better than God's, any table better than the Lord's, any person better than your Savior, anyone better than your soul, a present indulgence better than the hope of heaven—take alarm! —GUTHRIE

AUGUST 15

By faith Noah...prepared an ark to
the saving of his house.
—Hebrews 11:7

What a humble, what a modest sphere for the exercise of faith! One would have said that the purpose was quite disproportionate to the work. The ark was a great undertaking, but what was it undertaken for? To save his own family. Is so narrow a sphere worthy to be the object of faith? Is so commonplace a scene as the life of the family circle fit to be a temple for the service of God?

My soul, when you have finished your prayers and ended your meditations, do not say that you have left the house of God. God's house will to you be everywhere, and your own house will be a part of it. You will feel that all the duties of this place are consecrated; that it is none other than the house of God and one of the gates to heaven. You will feel that every one of its duties is an act of high communion. Therefore it is yours to make your house His house. It is yours to consecrate each word and look and deed in the social life of home. It is yours to build your ark or refuge for the wants of common days; truly, your labor of love will be called an act of faith. —GEORGE MATHESON

AUGUST 16

Be ye followers of me, even as I also am of Christ.
—1 Corinthians 11:1

When in the Mexican war the troops were wavering, a general rose in his stirrups and dashed into the enemy's line, shouting, "Men, follow!" They seeing his courage and disposition, dashed on after him, and gained the victory. What men need to rally them for God is an example to lead them. All your commands to others to advance amount to nothing as long as you stay behind. To effect them aright, you need to start for heaven yourself, looking back only to give the stirring cry of "Men, follow!" —T. DEWITT TALMAGE

AUGUST 17

And Jesus went forth, and saw a great multitude, and was moved with compassion toward them, and he healed their sick....And when he had sent the multitudes away, he went up into a mountain apart to pray: and when the evening was come, he was there alone.
—Matthew 14:14, 23

Do we, like Him, combine the two great elements of human character? Are our public duties, the cares, the business and engrossments of the world finely tempered and hallowed by a secret walk with God? If the world were to follow us from its busy thoroughfares, would it trace us to our family altars and our closet devotions?

Action and meditation are the two great components of Christian life, and the perfection of the religious character is to find the two in unison and harmony. —MACDUFF

AUGUST 18

Nevertheless at thy word.
—Luke 5:5

Oh, what a blessed formula for us! This path of mine is dark, mysterious, perplexing; "nevertheless, at Your word" I will go forward. This trial of mine is cutting sore for flesh and blood to bear. It is hard to breathe through a broken heart, "Your will be done." But, "nevertheless, at Your word," I will say, "Even so, Father!" (Matthew 11:26). This besetting habit, or infirmity, or sin of mine is difficult to crucify. It has become part of myself—a second nature. To be severed from it would be like the cutting off of a right hand, or the plucking out of a right eye; "nevertheless, at Your word," I will lay aside every weight. This idol I will utterly abolish. This righteousness of mine is hard to ignore: all these virtues, and amiabilities, and natural graces—it is hard to believe that they do not dare in any way to be mixed up in the matter of my salvation, and that I am to receive all from first to last as the gift of God, through Jesus Christ my Lord. "Nevertheless, at Your word," I will count all but loss for the excellency of His knowledge. —MACDUFF

AUGUST 19

I am the LORD, I change not.
—Malachi 3:6

Our hope is not hung upon such untwisted thread as "I imagine so," or "It is likely." Rather, the cable, the strong rope of our fastened anchor, is the oath and promise of Him who is eternal truth. Our salvation is fastened with God's own hand and Christ's own strength to the strong stake of God's unchanging nature.　　　—WILLIAM RUTHERFORD

AUGUST 20

My grace is sufficient for thee: for my strength is made perfect in weakness.
—2 Corinthians 12:9

God's way of answering His people's prayers is not by removing pressure, but by increasing their strength to bear it. The pressure is often the fence between the narrow way of life and the broad road to ruin: if our heavenly Father removed it, it might be at the sacrifice of heaven. If God had removed that thorny fence in answer to earnest prayers, so many of us would now be castaways! The song of many a saint now in glory would be hushed! Many a harp would be unstrung! Many a place in the mansions of the redeemed would be empty! If God answered all the prayers we put up to heaven, we would need no other scourge. Blessed it is that we have One who is too loving to grant what we so rashly ask. —F. WHITFIELD

AUGUST 21

Abide in me, and I in you. As the branch cannot bear fruit of itself, except it abide in the vine; no more can ye, except ye abide in me.
—John 15:4

From moment to moment, and from hour to hour, the inner nature of man is to be continuously sustained with the life of God. Only as I am constantly receiving His fullness into my emptiness am I really living in the true, full, deep sense of the word, that life of eternity, which is my privilege now, and will be my glory hereafter.
—W. HAY AITKEN

AUGUST 22

Let the peace of God rule in your hearts.
—Colossians 3:15

Years ago one of our fleets was terribly shattered by a violent gale, but it was found that some of the ships were unaffected by its violence. They were in what mariners call "the eye of the storm." While all around was desolation, they were safe. So it is with all those who have the peace of God in their hearts. —PILKINGTON

AUGUST 23

Serving the Lord with all humility of mind.
—Acts 20:19

There is a legend of an artist who long sought for a piece of sandalwood, out of which to carve a Madonna. He was about to give up in despair, leaving the vision of his life unrealized, when in a dream he was bidden to carve his Madonna from a block of oak wood which was destined for the fire. He obeyed and produced a masterpiece from a log of common firewood.

Many of us lose great opportunities in life by waiting to find sandalwood for our carvings, when they really lie hidden in the common logs that we burn.   —ORISON SWETT MARDEN

AUGUST 24

I will cause the shower to come down in his season;
there shall be showers of blessing.
—Ezekiel 34:26

What is your season this morning? Is it the season of drought? Then that is the season for showers. Is it a season of great heaviness and black clouds? Then that is the season for showers. *"As thy days, so shall thy strength be"* (Deuteronomy 33:25). I will give you *"showers of blessing."* The word is in the plural. All kinds of blessings God will send. All God's blessings go together, like links in a golden chain. If He gives converting grace, He will also give comforting grace.

AUGUST

He will send *"showers of blessings."* Look up today, O parched plant, and open your leaves and flowers for a heavenly watering. —SPURGEON

AUGUST 25

If we suffer, we shall also reign with him.
—2 Timothy 2:12

The photographer must have a negative, as he calls it, in order to furnish you with a picture. Now, the earthly cross is the negative from which the heavenly crown is to be made, the suffering and sorrow of the present time determining the glory, honor and immortality of the life to come. —A. J. GORDON

AUGUST 26

Love not the world, neither the things
that are in the world.
—1 John 2:15

If you will go to the banks of a little stream and watch the flies that come to bathe in it, you will notice that, while they plunge their bodies into the water, they keep their wings high out of the water; and, after swimming about a little while, they fly away with their wings unwet through the sunny air. Now, that is the lesson for us. Here we are immersed in the cares and business of the world; but let us keep the wings of our soul, our faith and our love, out of the world so that, with these unclogged, we may be ready to take our flight to heaven. —J. INGLIS

AUGUST 27

I would have you without carefulness.
—1 Corinthians 7:32

Do not look forward to the changes and chances of this life in fear. Rather look to them with full hope that, as they arise, God, whose you are, will deliver you out of them. He has kept you until now. Do but hold fast to His dear hand, and He will lead you safely through all things; and when you cannot stand, He will bear you in His arms. Do not look forward to what may happen tomorrow. The same everlasting Father who cares for you today will take care of you tomorrow and every day. Either He will shield you from suffering, or He will give you unfailing strength to bear it. Be at peace then, and put aside all anxious thoughts and imaginations.

—FRANCES DE SALES

AUGUST 28

Leaving you an example, that ye should
follow his steps.
—1 Peter 2:21 ASV

I have long since ceased to pray, "Lord Jesus, have compassion on a lost world!" I remember the day and the hour when I seemed to hear the Lord rebuking me for making such a prayer. He seemed to say to me, "I have had compassion upon a lost world, and now it is for you to have compassion."

—A. J. GORDON

AUGUST 29

We are his workmanship, created in Christ Jesus
unto good works, which God hath before
ordained that we should walk in them.
—Ephesians 2:10

No man is born into the world whose work is not born with him. There is always work, and tools to work with, for those who will.

—J. R. LOWELL

AUGUST 30

Ye call me, Teacher, and, Lord:
and ye say well; for so I am.
—John 13:13 ASV

How wonderful a Teacher we have! Sometimes we seek Him in the house, but He is not there. We go forth seeking Him and find Him perhaps in the wilderness or on a mountain praying, or leading some poor blind man by the hand, or eating with publicans or sinners, or asleep in a storm, or conversing with a Samaritan woman, or surrounded by wrathful men, or bearing a cross. It is not merely His words that instruct. His place, His occupation, His companions, His environment, His garment, His silence, His submission—all teem with instruction. And they that learn of Him are made like Him.

—GEORGE BOWEN

AUGUST 31

Ye serve the Lord Christ.
—Colossians 3:24

Our business as Christians is to serve the Lord in every business of life. —MARK GUY PEARSE

SEPTEMBER

SEPTEMBER 1

Thus saith the Lord God; I will yet for this be inquired
of by the house of Israel, to do it for them.
—Ezekiel 36:37

Prayer is the forerunner of mercy. Turn to sacred history, and you will find that scarcely ever did a great mercy come to the world unheralded by supplication. Prayer is always the preface to blessing, preceding the blessing as its shadow. When the sunlight of God's mercy rises on our necessities, it casts the shadow of prayer far down upon the plain. Or, to use another illustration, when God piles up a hill of mercies, He Himself shines behind them, and He casts on our spirits the shadow of prayer. We may rest certain, if we are much in prayer, that our pleadings are the shadows of mercy. Prayer is connected with blessing to show us its value.

—SPURGEON

SEPTEMBER 2

I have chosen thee in the furnace of affliction.
—Isaiah 48:10

Does not the word come like a soft shower, assuaging the fury of the flame? Yes, is it not an asbestos armor, against which the heat has no power? Let affliction come—God has chosen me. Poverty, you may stride in at my door—but God is in the house already, and He has chosen me. Sickness, you may intrude, but I have a balsam ready—God has chosen me. Whatever befalls me in this vale of tears, I know that He has chosen me. Fear not, Christian, for Jesus is with you. In all your fiery trials His presence is both your comfort and safety. He will never leave one whom He has chosen for His own. *"Fear not, for I am with thee"* (Genesis 26:24), is His sure word of promise to His chosen ones in the *"furnace of affliction."*   —SPURGEON

SEPTEMBER 3

In the daytime...he led them with a cloud, and all the night with a light of fire.
—Psalm 78:14

My day is my prosperity; it is the time when the sun of fortune is bright above me, and, therefore, it is the time when I need a shade. If my sunshine were not checkered I would forget You, O my God.

But I have nights to meet, as well as days. The night is my adversity; it is the time when the sun of fortune has gone down behind the hills, and I am left alone. Then it is, O my Father, that I need the light of Your fire! My light for the night is the vision of Calvary—the vision of Your love in the cross. I need the light of Your fire *"all the night."*

—GEORGE MATHESON

SEPTEMBER 4

It is high time to awake out of sleep.
—Romans 13:11

I have heard of a painter who loved to work by the morning light. He said that the colors were better understood by the light of the early day, and so he wanted to be in his studio waiting for the rising of the sun. Then every moment it grew lighter, and he found he could accomplish things that he could not reach if he waited until the day had advanced.

Is there not work waiting for us—work that no one else can do—work, too, that the Master has promised to help us perform? Will He come and find that we still sleep? Or will the Son of Righteousness, when He appears, find us waiting, as that painter waited, looking and longing for the first gleam of day? Surely those of us who thus wait on the Lord will renew our strength, and, eagle-like, rise to greet the Son.

—THOMAS CHAMPNESS

SEPTEMBER 5

Let us not be weary in well doing: for in due season
we shall reap, if we faint not.
—Galatians 6:9

The hours of this present life are the ages in embryo of the life to come. —A. J. GORDON

SEPTEMBER 6

Now are we the sons of God, and it doth not yet
appear what we shall be: but we know that, when he
shall appear, we shall be like him; for we shall
see him as he is.
—1 John 3:2

"Now are we the sons of God." That is the pier upon one side of the gulf. *"It doth not yet appear what we shall be: but...when he shall appear, we shall be like him."* That is the pier on the other. How are the two to be connected? There is only one way by which the present sonship will blossom and fruit into the future perfect likness, and that is, if we throw across the gulf, by God's help day by day, the bridge of growing likeness to Himself, and purity therefrom. —ALEXANDER MACLAREN

SEPTEMBER 7

The church of God, which he hath purchased
with his own blood.
—Acts 20:28

Surely He may do what He will with His own. The price He has paid to make them His own is a sufficient guarantee that He will never make light of anything in which their welfare is at all concerned. We are precious to Him by the virtue of the blood that he has shed for us, and for Him to be found at any time wanting in solicitude for our happiness would be for Him to treat that blood of His as the sinners of this world treat it. The persuasion of Christ's love must be engraved in our hearts so deeply that no semblance of indifference on His part will ever make the slightest impression upon us. This is the victory that overcomes the world.

—GEORGE BOWEN

SEPTEMBER 8

He asked life of thee, and thou gavest it him, even length of days for ever and ever.
—Psalm 21:4

When poor men make requests of us, we usually answer them as the echo does the voice—the answer cuts off half the petition. We will seldom find Jael's courtesy among men, giving milk to those that ask water, except it be as this was, an entangling benefit, the better to introduce a mischief. There are not many Naamans among us, that, when you beg of them one talent, will force you to take two; but God's answer to our prayers is like a multiplying glass, which renders the request much greater in the answer than it was in the prayer.

—BISHOP REYNOLDS

SEPTEMBER 9

This beginning of miracles did Jesus.
—John 2:11

It was out of the common thing that the precious thing was brought; and it is out of the common things of daily life, presented obediently to Jesus and laid at His feet, that He brings His own glorious gifts, so that our whole lives become one great sacrament. —W. HAY AITKEN

SEPTEMBER 10

The God of hope fill you with all joy and peace in believing, that ye may abound in hope, through the power of the Holy Ghost.
—Romans 15:13

In spiritual as in earthly things there is great strength in hope, and, therefore, God's people are to cultivate that grace carefully. A well-grounded hope that, having been made new creatures in Jesus Christ, we are His; that with our names, though unknown to fame, written in the Book of Life, we have grace in possession and heaven in prospect; that after a few more brief years, pure as the angels that sing before the throne, we will be brought with gladness into the palace of the King, to be like Christ and with Christ, seeing Him eye to eye and face to face—such hopes are powerful springs of action. —GUTHRIE

SEPTEMBER 11

The life which I now live in the flesh.
—Galatians 2:20

I expect to pass through this world but once. Therefore, if there be any kindness I can show or any good thing I can do to any fellow human being, let me do it now; let me not defer or neglect it, for I will not pass this way again.   —MARCUS AURELIUS

SEPTEMBER 12

Base things of the world, and things which are despised, hath God chosen.
—1 Corinthians 1:28

In some of the great halls of Europe may be seen pictures not painted with the brush, but mosaics, which are made up of small pieces of stone, glass, or other material. The artist takes these little pieces, and, polishing and arranging them, he forms them into the grand and beautiful picture. Each individual part of the picture may be a little worthless piece of glass or marble or shell; but, with each in its place, the whole constitutes the masterpiece of art.

So I think it will be with humanity in the hands of the great Artist. God is picking up the little worthless pieces of stone and brass that might be trodden under foot unnoticed, and is making of them His great masterpiece.   —BISHOP SIMPSON

SEPTEMBER 13

*I will instruct thee and teach thee in the way which
thou shalt go: I will guide thee with mine eye.*
—Psalm 32:8

When God does the directing, our life is useful
and full of promise, whatever it is doing; and discipline has its perfecting work.   —H. E. COBB

SEPTEMBER 14

*When thou prayest, enter into thy closet, and when
thou hast shut thy door, pray to thy Father
which is in secret.*
—Matthew 6:6

This is faith's stronghold; here she arms herself
for the daily conflict. Silence in that closet of prayer
speaks death throughout all the house. When that
door is suffered to rust on its hinges and that
chamber is deserted, then the heart-house is soon
retaken by Satan, and evil spirits come in and dwell
there.   —THEODORE CUYLER

SEPTEMBER 15

Jesus...went about doing good.
—Acts 10:38

The finest of all fine arts is the art of doing
good; and yet it is the least cultivated.
—T. DEWITT TALMAGE

SEPTEMBER 16

Behold, we go up to Jerusalem.
—Matthew 20:18

Never had there been such a going up to Jerusalem as that which Jesus here proposes to His disciples. He goes up voluntarily. The act was not enforced by any external compulsion. Jerusalem might at this time have been avoided. It was deliberately sought. It was a going up to a triumph to be reached through defeat, a coronation to be attained through ignominy and humiliation. O believer, in your walk through the world today, be strengthened, be comforted, be inspired by the spectacle of the Captain of your salvation thus going up to Jerusalem! And remember, in all those apparently downward passages of life where sorrow and maybe death lie before you, that all such descents, made or endured in the Spirit of Jesus, are really upgoing steps, leading you to the mount of God and the resurrection glory.　　　—J. B. STRATTON

SEPTEMBER 17

And the angel of the Lord said unto her [Hagar],
Return to thy mistress, and submit thyself
under her hands.
—Genesis 16:9

Submission is a great Christian law, but we find it early in Genesis, early in the history of mankind, and angel-given.　　　—SELECTED

151

SEPTEMBER 18

Wait for the promise of the Father.
—Acts 1:4

Tarry at a promise until God meets you there. He always returns by way of His promises.
—SELECTED

SEPTEMBER 19

Then spake Solomon,...I have surely built
thee an house to dwell in.
—1 Kings 8:12–13

Only Solomon, the prince of peace, could build the temple. If we would be soulwinners and build up the church, which is God's temple, let us note this; not by discussion nor by argument, but by lifting up Jesus Christ will we draw men unto Him.
—J. HUDSON TAYLOR

SEPTEMBER 20

These were the potters, and those that dwelt
among plants and hedges: there they dwelt
with the king for his work.
—1 Chronicles 4:23

Anywhere and everywhere we may dwell *"with the king for his work."* We may be in a very unlikely or unfavorable place for this; it may be in a little country life, with little enough to be seen of the "goings" of the King around us; it may be among hedges of all sorts, hindrances in all directions; it may be, furthermore, with our hands full of all manner of pottery for our daily task. No matter! The King who placed us *"there"* will come and dwell there with us; the hedges are all right, or He would soon do away with them; and it does not follow that what seems to hinder our way may not be for its very protection; and as for the pottery, why, this is just exactly what He has seen fit to put into our hands, and therefore it is, for the present, *"His work."*   —FRANCES RIDLEY HAVERGAL

SEPTEMBER 21

Be ye holy; for I am holy.
—1 Peter 1:16

The highway of holiness is along the common-est road of life—along your very way. In wind and rain, no matter how it beats—it is only going hand in hand with Him.   —MARK GUY PEARSE

SEPTEMBER 22

And the LORD said, Shall I hide from Abraham that thing which I do?
—Genesis 18:17

Abraham, in communion with God, knew long before Lot, in Sodom, of the destruction of that city. Oh, for more communion!   —SELECTED

SEPTEMBER 23

The Son of man came not to be ministered unto, but to minister, and to give his life a ransom for many.
—Matthew 20:28

We are to surrender ourselves to Christ so that this great purpose of His coming will claim and possess the whole life. We are to live, like God, to bless others. This is His will, His purpose concerning us. This is what His power waits to do for us. This is the claim of His great love upon us. Do not assent to the truth of it and then pass by neglectfully on the other side. Do not think and pray about it without even a passing hope that your prayer will be answered. Do not gather yourself up in great resolutions to be good and useful. Kneel in sight of the Crucified. In the cross of Christ, spell out His great purpose and yearning love to men. Let the heart feel all the might of the appeal that comes to us from His torn hands and feet and bleeding brow, from all the dreadful shame and agony of our dear Lord. Bought and bound by all this, surrender yourself to Him for His great purpose. Take Him as your strength for this work.

—MARK GUY PEARSE

SEPTEMBER 24

So teach us to number our days, that we may apply our hearts unto wisdom.
—Psalm 90:12

Every day is a little life, and our whole life is but a day repeated. Whence it is that old Jacob numbers his life by days, and Moses desires to be taught this point of holy arithmetic—to number not his years, but his days. Those, therefore, that dare lose a day are dangerously prodigal; those that dare misspend it, desperate. —BISHOP HALL

SEPTEMBER 25

This is the victory that overcometh the world, even our faith.
—1 John 5:4

The world conquers me when it succeeds in hindering me from seeing, loving, holding communion with, and serving my Father God. I conquer it when I lay my hand upon it and force it to help me to get nearer Him, to get more like Him, to think oftener of Him, to do His will more gladly and more constantly. The one victory over the world is to bend it to serve me in the highest things—the attainment of a clearer vision of the divine nature, the attainment of a deeper love to God Himself, and a gladder consecration and service to Him. That is the victory—when you can make the world a ladder to lift you to God. When the world comes between you and God as an obscuring screen, it has conquered you. When the world comes between you and God as a transparent medium, you have conquered it. To win victory is to get it beneath your feet and stand upon it, and reach up thereby to God. —ALEXANDER MACLAREN

SEPTEMBER 26

Christ in you, the hope of glory.
—Colossians 1:27

Religion is not the simple fire escape that you build upon the outside of your dwelling, in anticipation of a possible danger, and leave there until danger comes. You go to it some morning when a fire breaks out in your house, and the poor old thing that you built up there, and thought that you could use some day, is so rusty and broken, and the weather has so beaten upon it, and the sun so turned its hinges, that it will not work. That is the condition of a man who has built himself what seems a creed of faith, a trust in God in anticipation of the day when danger is to overtake him, and has said to himself, "I am safe, for I will take refuge in it then." But religion is the house in which we live, it is the table at which we sit, it is the fireside at which we draw near, the room that arches its graceful and familiar presence over us. It is the bed on which we lie and think of the past, anticipate the future, and gather our refreshment.

—PHILLIPS BROOKS

SEPTEMBER 27

Serve the LORD with gladness: come before his presence with singing.
—Psalm 100:2

God wants our lives to be a song. He has written the music for us in His Word and in the duties that come to us in our places and relations in life. The things we ought to do are the notes set upon the staff. To make our life beautiful music, we must be obedient and submissive. Any disobedience is the singing of a false note and yields discord.

—J. R. MILLER

SEPTEMBER 28

To the Lord our God belong
mercies and forgivenesses.
—Daniel 9:9

As a spring lock closes itself, but cannot be unlocked without a key, so we ourselves may run into sin, but cannot return without the key of God's grace. —CAWDRAY

SEPTEMBER 29

He shall give his angels charge over thee,
to keep thee in all thy ways.
—Psalm 91:11

Count no duty too little, no round of life too small, no work too low, if it comes in your way, since God thinks so much of it as to send His angels to guard you in it. —MARK GUY PEARSE

SEPTEMBER 30

My presence shall go with thee.
—Exodus 33:14

We should never leave our prayer closets in the morning without having focused our thoughts deeply and intensely on the fact of the actual presence of God there with us, encompassing us, and filling the room as literally as it fills heaven itself. It may not lead to any distinct results at first, but, as we make repeated efforts to realize the presence of God, it will become increasingly real to us. And, as the habit grows upon us, when alone in a room, or when treading the lawn of some natural woodland temple, or when pacing the stony street—in the silence of night or amid the teeming crowds of daylight—we will often find ourselves whispering the words, "You are near. You are here, O Lord."

—F. B. MEYER

O C T O B E R

OCTOBER 1

Surely he shall deliver thee from the snare
of the fowler.
—Psalm 91:3

"He shall deliver thee from the snare of the fowler." That means from the little things, the hidden traps and nets that are set for us. Great sins frighten, but little snares entangle. It is easier to escape the huntsman's arrow than the crafty lure.

And where are they not set? Riches and poverty, sickness and strength, prosperity and adversity, friendship and loneliness, the work and the lack of it—each has its snare, wherein not only are the unwary caught, but the wise and the watchful sometimes fall prey. Little things, mere threads, hardly worth guarding against—yet they are strong enough to hold us and hinder us, and may be the beginning of our destruction. —MARK GUY PEARSE

OCTOBER 2

God is love; and he that dwelleth in love dwelleth in God, and God in him.
—1 John 4:16

It is good and true to think that every ray of the sun touching the earth has the sun at the other end of it. Just so, every bit of love upon God's earth has God at the other end of it.   —MARK GUY PEARSE

OCTOBER 3

At Jesus' feet.
—Luke 10:39

"At Jesus' feet" is our place of privilege and of blessing. Here it is that we are to be educated and fitted for the practical duties of life. Here we are to renew our strength while we wait on Him and to learn how to mount up with wings as eagles; here we are to become possessed of that true knowledge that is power; and here we are to learn how real work is done and to be armed with the true motive power to do it. Here we are to find solace amid both the trials of work—and they are not few—and the trials of life in general. Here we are to anticipate something of the blessedness of heaven amid the days of earth, for to sit at His feet is indeed to be in heavenly places, and to gaze upon His glory is to do what we will never tire of doing yonder.

—W. HAY AITKEN

OCTOBER 4

Be not afraid, only believe.
—Mark 5:36

Do not be downcast if difficulties and trials surround you in your heavenly life. They may be purposely placed there by God to train and discipline you for higher developments of faith. If He calls you to "toiling in rowing," it may be to make you the hardier seaman, to lead you to lift up the hands that hang down, and the feeble knees, and, above all, to drive you to a holier trust in Him who has the vessel and its destinies in His hand, and who, amid gathering clouds and darkened horizon and crested billows, is ever uttering the mild rebuke to our misgivings—*"Said I not unto thee, that if thou wouldest believe, thou shouldest see the glory of God?"* (John 11:40).   —MACDUFF

OCTOBER 5

Happy is the man whom God correcteth.
—Job 5:17

Happy, because the correction is designed to bring him into paths of blessedness and peace. Happy, because there is no unnecessary severity in it. Happy, because the chastisement is not so much against us as against our most cruel enemies—our sins. Happy, because we have abundant words of consolation. Happy, because whom the Lord loves He chastens. Happy, because our light affliction is but for a moment.   —GEORGE BOWEN

OCTOBER 6

I spake unto thee in thy prosperity.
—Jeremiah 22:21

We shade our eyes with the hand to shut out the glare of the strong daylight when we want to see far away. God thus puts, as it were, His hand upon our brows, and tempers the glow of prosperity, that we may take in the wider phases of His goodness. It is a common experience that, looking out from the gloom of some personal affliction, men have seen for the first time beyond the earth plane, and caught glimpses of the Beulah Land. Let us not shrink from the Hand that we know is heavy only with blessing. —LUDLOW

OCTOBER 7

When I sit in darkness, the LORD shall be a light unto me.
—Micah 7:8

If you are willing to choose the seeming darkness of faith instead of the illumination of reason, wonderful light will break out upon you from the Word of God. —A. J. GORDON

OCTOBER 8

When they saw the star, they rejoiced with exceeding great joy.
—Matthew 2:10

We who look for Jesus ought to be joyful; it is no credit to our Lord when we look as though we were seeking His grave. The dull looks of Christ's followers have injured Him in the sight of the world. Let us, then, smile as we go, for we have the star if we look upward and put ourselves in the right path.

—THOMAS CHAMPNESS

OCTOBER 9

Who is among you that feareth the LORD,...that walketh in darkness, and hath no light? let him trust in the name of the LORD, and stay upon his God.
—Isaiah 50:10

"In fierce storms," said an old seaman, "we can do but one thing; there is only one way. We must put the ship in a certain position and keep her there."

This, Christian, is what you must do. Sometimes, like Paul, you can see neither sun nor stars, and no small tempest lies on you. Then you can do but one thing: there is only one way. Reason cannot help you. Past experiences give you no light. Even prayer fetches no consolation. Only a single course is left. You must put your soul in one position and keep it there. You must stay upon the Lord. Come what may—winds, waves, lightning, thunder, frowning rocks, roaring breakers—you must lash yourself to the helm and hold fast your confidence in God's faithfulness, His sovereign engagement, His everlasting love in Christ Jesus.   —RICHARD FULLER

OCTOBER 10

*O Lord G*ᴏᴅ*, thou knowest.*
—Ezekiel 37:3

Here is the response of faith, "You know!" What a pillow for the heart to repose upon! "You know!" What few but comprehensive words to sum up and express the heart's difficulties and perplexities and trials. "You know!" What an inexpressibly sweet resting place in the midst of life's tumultuous heavings, in the midst of a sea that knows no calm, in the midst of a scene in which tossings to and fro are the hourly history! What an answer they contain for every heart that can find no words to express its big emotions, for a heart whose sorrows are too deep for language to find its way to God! Oh, that they were ever uppermost in the soul, as the response to every difficulty in our path! They are God's answer to everything we cannot fathom, God's answer for our hearts to rest upon and our lips to utter when every way is hedged up so that we cannot pass. "O Lord God, You know!" Rest here, believer. Lean your soul on these words. Repose calmly on the bosom of your God, and carry them with you into every scene of life. "O Lord God, You know."

—F. WHITFIELD

OCTOBER 11

Come and dine.
—John 21:12

This morning the voice of the Beloved of our soul is heard giving us His invitation. "Children," He asks, "have you any meat?"

We answer, "No, of ourselves we have nothing but hunger and starvation. O God, we cannot feed ourselves!"

Then it is that His own sweet voice replies, "Come and dine!" —W. HAY AITKEN

OCTOBER 12

I live; yet not I, but Christ liveth in me: and the life which I now live in the flesh I live by the faith of the Son of God, who loved me, and gave himself for me.
—Galatians 2:20

The man who lives in God knows no life except the life of God. —PHILLIPS BROOKS

OCTOBER 13

The word of our God shall stand for ever.
—Isaiah 40:8

The Word of God is the water of life: the more freely you allow it to flow, the fresher it runs. It is the fire of God's glory: the more you blow on it, the clearer it burns. It is the corn of the Lord's field: the better you grind it, the more it yields. It is the bread of heaven: the more it is broken and given forth, the more it remains. It is the sword of the Spirit: the more it is used, the brighter it shines.

—BISHOP JEWEL

OCTOBER 14

Surely the LORD is in this place; and I knew it not.
—Genesis 28:16

The parish priest, of austerity,
   Climbed up in the high church steeple
To be nearer God, that he might hand
   His word down to the people.
And in sermon script he daily wrote
   What he thought was sent from heaven;
And he dropped it down on the people's heads
   Two times one day in seven.
In his age God said, "Come down and die."
   And he cried out from the steeple:
"Where art Thou, Lord?" And the Lord replied:
   "Down here among My people."
                —AUTHOR UNKNOWN

OCTOBER 15

Now therefore hearken, O Israel, unto the statutes and
unto the judgments, which I teach you, for to do them,
that ye may live, and go in and possess the land which
the LORD God of your fathers giveth you.
—Deuteronomy 4:1

   "Hearken" and *"do,"* that ye may *"live"* and *"possess."* This is a universal and abiding principle. It was true for Israel, and it is true for us. The pathway of life and the true secret of possession is simple obedience to the holy commandments of God. We see this all through the inspired volume, from cover to cover. God has given us His Word,

not to speculate upon it or discuss it, but that we may obey it. And it is as we, through grace, yield a hearty and happy obedience to our Father's statutes and judgments, that we tread the bright pathway of life, and enter into the reality of all that God has treasured up for us in Christ.   —C. H. M.

OCTOBER 16

He riseth from supper, and laid aside his garments; and took a towel, and girded himself. After that he poureth water into a basin, and began to wash the disciples' feet, and to wipe them with the towel wherewith he was girded.
—John 13:4–5

Acts are common and humiliating because they are ordinarily expressive of the thoughts of men. Let us not accuse the acts that make up our daily lives of meanness, but our ignoble souls that reveal themselves so unworthily through those acts. The same act may successively mount up through every intermediate stage from the depth of unworthiness to a transcendent height of excellence, according to the soul that is manifested by it. One of the glorious ends of our Lord's incarnation was that He might repair us using the details of life, so that we would not disdain these as insignificant, but rather disdain ourselves for our inability to make these details interpreters of a noble nature. Oh, let us then look with affectionateness and gratitude upon the daily details of life, seeing the sanctifying imprint of the hand of Jesus upon them all!   —GEORGE BOWEN

OCTOBER 17

*Behold a ladder set up on the earth, and the top of it
reached to heaven.*
—Genesis 28:12

Think of that mystic ladder, which descends from the throne of God to the spot, however lowly, where you may be. It may be a moorland waste, a humble cottage, a ship's cabin, a settler's hut, a bed of pain, but Jesus Christ finds you out and comes just where you are. The one pole of this ladder is the gold of His deity; the other is the silver of His manhood. The rungs are the series of events from the cradle of Bethlehem to the right hand of power where He sits. That ladder sways beneath a weight of blessing for you. Oh, that you would send away your burdens of sin, care, and fear by the hands of the ascending angels of prayer and faith, so that you would be able to receive into your heart the trooping angels of peace, joy, love, and glory.

—F. B. MEYER

OCTOBER 18

*They took knowledge of them,
that they had been with Jesus.*
—Acts 4:13

A Christian should be a striking likeness of Jesus Christ. You have read lives of Christ, beautifully and eloquently written, but the best life of

Christ is His living biography, written out in the words and actions of His people. If we were what we profess to be, and what we should be, we would be pictures of Christ; yes, such striking likenesses of Him that the world would not have to hold us up and say, "Well, it seems somewhat a likeness," but they would, when they once beheld us, exclaim, "He has been with Jesus; he has been taught of Him; he is like Him; he has caught the very idea of the holy Man of Nazareth, and he works it out in his life and everyday actions." —SPURGEON

OCTOBER 19

As my lord the king hath said, so will thy servant do.
—1 Kings 2:38

There is something infinitely better than doing a great thing for God, and the infinitely better thing is to be where God wants us to be, to do what God wants us to do, and to have no will apart from His.
—G. CAMPBELL MORGAN

OCTOBER 20

I [Daniel] *was left alone, and saw this great vision.*
—Daniel 10:8

Solitude is the antechamber of God; only one step more and you can be in His immediate presence. —LANDOR

OCTOBER 21

That the God of our Lord Jesus Christ, the Father of
glory, may give unto you the spirit of wisdom and
revelation in the knowledge of him: the eyes of your
understanding being enlightened.
—Ephesians 1:17–18

We were coming down a mountain in Switzerland one evening, when a black thunderstorm blotted out the day, and all was suddenly plunged into darkness. We could only dimly see the narrow, dusty footpaths, and the gloomy sides that were swallowed up in deeper gloom. What then of the majesty all about us—heights, and depths, and wonders? All was darkness. Then came the lightning—not flashes, but the blazing of the whole sky—incessant, and on every side. What recesses of glory we gazed into! What marvels of splendor shone out of the darkness!

Think how with us, in us, is One who comes to make the common, dusty ways of life resplendent, illuminating our dull thoughts by the light of the glory of God; clearing the vision of the soul, and then revealing the greatness of the salvation that is ours in Christ.   —MARK GUY PEARSE

OCTOBER 22

The eleven disciples went...into a mountain where
Jesus had appointed them....Jesus came and spake
unto them, saying,...Go ye...and teach all nations.
—Matthew 28:16, 18–19

OCTOBER

The considerable actions in the world have usually very small beginnings. Of a few letters, how many thousand words are made! Of ten figures, how many thousand numbers! A point is the beginning of all geometry. A little stone flung into a pond makes a little circle, then a greater, until it enlarges itself to the sides. So from small beginnings God causes an efflux through the whole world. —CHARNOCK

OCTOBER 23

Whom the Lord loveth he chasteneth.
—Hebrews 12:6

Earthly prosperity is no sign of the special love of heaven, nor are sorrow and care any mark of God's disfavor. God's love is robust, true, and eager—not for our comfort, but for our lasting blessedness. It is bent on achieving this, and it is strong enough to bear misrepresentation and rebuke in its attempts to attune our spirits to higher music. It comes instructing us. Let us enter ourselves as pupils in the school of God's love. Let us lay aside our own notions of the course of study; let us submit ourselves to be led and taught; let us be prepared for any lessons that may be given from the blackboard of sorrow; let us be so assured of the inexhaustible tenacity of His love as to dare to trust Him, though He slay us. And let us look forward to that august moment when He will give us a reason for all life's discipline, with a smile that will thrill our souls with ecstasy and constrain sorrow and sighing to flee away forever. —F. B. MEYER

OCTOBER 24

Flee into Egypt.
—Matthew 2:13

Why? Because there is a cruel king who will seek the young child's life.

Is Christ born in you? Is your life like that manger—precious as a casket, because of what it holds? Then have a care; for, craftier and more unscrupulous than Herod, the destroyer of souls will seek to destroy you. There is a day coming when they will say, *"They are dead which sought the young child's life"* (Matthew 2:20). Grace will survive the foe, and we will yet return to enjoy the comforts of life, with no Herod to threaten us. After all, it is sin that is short-lived, for goodness will flourish when the evil one is chained up forever.

—THOMAS CHAMPNESS

OCTOBER 25

He placed...Cherubims, and a flaming sword...to keep
the way of the tree of life.
—Genesis 3:24

Blessed are they that do his commandments, that they
may have right to the tree of life.
—Revelation 22:14

How remarkable and beautiful it is that the last pages of Revelation should bend round to touch the first pages of Genesis! The history of man began with angels with frowning faces and flaming swords barring the way to the Tree of Life. It ends with the cherubim guards withdrawn; or perhaps, sheathing their swords and becoming guides to the no longer forbidden fruit, instead of being its guards. That is the Bible's grand symbolic way of saying that all between—the sin, the misery, the death—is a parenthesis. God's purpose is not going to be thwarted. The end of His majestic march through history is to be men's access to the Tree of Life, from which, for the dreary ages that are but as a moment in the great eternities, they were barred out by sin. —ALEXANDER MACLAREN

OCTOBER 26

*Be thou faithful unto death, and I will give
thee a crown of life.*
—Revelation 2:10

There is a heaven at the end of every faithful Christian's journey. —CUYLER

OCTOBER 27

The LORD set a mark upon Cain.
—Genesis 4:15

We speak of the mark of Cain as if it was the mark of a curse. In reality it was the mark of God's mercy, a defense against his enemies.
—D. J. BURRELL

OCTOBER 28

Let your light so shine before men,
that they may see your good works,
and glorify your Father
which is in heaven.
—Matthew 5:16

They say the world has an eagle eye for anything inconsistent, an eye sharp to discover the vagaries and inconsistencies in the faulty and the unworthy. It has an eagle eye; but the eagle winks before the sun, and the burning iris of its eye shrinks abashed before the purity of noon. Let your light so shine before men that others, awed and charmed by the consistency of your godly life, may come to inquire and to say that you have been with Jesus.

—PUNSHON

OCTOBER 29

Whatsoever ye shall ask
the Father in my name,
he will give it you.
—John 16:23

Prayer must be based upon promise, but, thank God, His promises are always broader than our prayers! No fear of building inverted pyramids here, for Jesus Christ is the foundation.

—FRANCES RIDLEY HAVERGAL

OCTOBER 30

Let us, who are of the day, be sober, putting on the
breastplate of faith and love; and for an helmet,
the hope of salvation.
—1 Thessalonians 5:8

Faith, love, hope—these three form the defensive armor that guards the soul—and these three make self-control possible. Like a diver in his gear who is let down to the bottom of the wild, tumultuous ocean, so a man whose heart is girded by faith and love, and whose head is covered with the helmet of hope, may be dropped down into the wildest sea of temptation and of worldliness, and yet will walk dry and unharmed through the midst of its depths, and breathe air that comes from a world far above the restless currents. Faith will bring you into communication with all the power of God. Love will lead you into a region where all the temptations round you will be touched as by Ithuriel's spear, and will show their own foulness. Hope will turn away your eyes from looking at the tempting splendor around, and fix them upon the glories that are above. And so the reins will come into your hands in an altogether new manner, and you will be able to be king over your own nature in a fashion that you did not dream of before, if only you will trust in Christ and love Him, fixing your desires on the things above. Then you will be able to govern yourself, when you let Christ govern you.

—ALEXANDER MACLAREN

OCTOBER 31

Continue in prayer.
—Colossians 4:2

✓ Our prayers often resemble the mischievous tricks of town children, who knock at their neighbor's houses and then run away; we often knock at heaven's door and then run off into the spirit of the world. Instead of waiting for entrance to be granted, we act as if we were afraid of having our prayers answered. —WILLIAMS

N O V E M B E R

NOVEMBER 1

*Thou wilt show me the path of life: in thy presence
is fulness of joy; at thy right hand there are
pleasures for evermore.*
—Psalm 16:11

The man who walks along the path of life lives in the presence of the joy-giving God. Insofar as he is true to that path of life and wanders neither to the right hand nor to the left, his joy becomes deeper; he becomes partaker of the very fullness of joy in which God Himself lives, moves, and has His being. While such is his experience in the midst of all the trials of life, he has the privilege of looking forward to grander things in store for him, when that higher world will be reached and the shadows of time have passed away. *"At thy right hand,"* exclaimed the psalmist, *"there are pleasures for evermore."*　　　　　　　　　—W. HAY AITKEN

NOVEMBER 2

Not I, but Christ liveth in me.
—Galatians 2:20

The wonder of the life in Jesus is this—and you will find it so, and you have found it so, if you have ever taken your New Testament and tried to make it the rule of your daily life—that there is not a single action that you are called upon to do of which you need be or will be in any serious doubt for ten minutes as to what Jesus Christ, being here, would have you do under those circumstances and with the material upon which you are called to act. The soul that takes in Jesus' word, the soul that through the words of Jesus enters into the very person of Jesus, the soul that knows Him as its daily presence and its daily law never hesitates.

—PHILLIPS BROOKS

NOVEMBER 3

Ye are the temple of the living God; as God hath said, I will dwell in them, and walk in them.
—2 Corinthians 6:16

These temples were raised for Him. Let Him fill them so completely that, like the oriental temple of glass in the ancient legend, the temple will not be seen, but only the glorious sunlight, which not only shines into it, but through it, and the transparent walls are all unseen.   —A. B. SIMPSON

NOVEMBER 4

A daily rate for every day.
—2 Kings 25:30

The acts of breathing that I performed yesterday will not keep me alive today. I must continue to breathe afresh every moment, or animal life ceases. In like manner, yesterday's grace and spiritual strength must be renewed, and the Holy Spirit must continue to breathe on my soul from moment to moment in order for my enjoying the consolations, and for my working the works of God.

—TOPLADY

NOVEMBER 5

Let us cleanse ourselves from all filthiness of the flesh and spirit, perfecting holiness in the fear of God.
—2 Corinthians 7:1

The Tree of Life, according to some of the old rabbinical legends, lifted its branches by an indwelling motion, high above impure hands that were stretched to touch them. Until our hands are cleansed through faith in Jesus Christ, its richest fruit hangs unreachable, golden above our heads. The fullness of the life of heaven is only granted to those who, drawing near Jesus Christ by faith on earth, have thereby cleansed themselves from all filthiness of the flesh and of the spirit.

—ALEXANDER MACLAREN

NOVEMBER 6

*Jesus was left alone, and the woman
standing in the midst.*
—John 8:9

Alone with Jesus! What a sweet and holy spot!
What a blessed refuge to which the soul may take
itself from the charges of Satan, the accusations
of the world, and the sorrows of life! Sweet spot
for the heart to unfold itself to tell its hidden tale
in the ear of infinite love, tenderness, and compassion! Alone with Jesus! How different a front
would Christianity present to the world if the Lord's
people were oftener there! What humility, gentleness, and love would characterize all their dealings! What holinesss stamped on the very brow,
that all might read! What few judgments passed on
others, what many more on ourselves! What calmness and resignation and joyful submission to all
the Lord's dealings!

Be much alone with Jesus! Then will the pas-
sage to glory be one of sunshine, whether it be
through the portals of the grave or through the
clouds of heaven. —F. WHITFIELD

NOVEMBER 7

*He which stablisheth us...in Christ, and hath anointed
us, is God; who hath also sealed us, and given the
earnest of the Spirit in our hearts.*
—2 Corinthians 1:21–22

When a Christian is *"sealed"* by the Holy Ghost, *"sealed"* as the property of his Master, there will be no need to ask, "Whose image and superscription is this?" (see Luke 20:24) upon the *"sealed"* one. The King's, of course. Anyone can see the image.

Of what use is a "seal" if it cannot be seen?

Is the King's image visibly, permanently stamped upon us? It is on every Spirit-filled, *"sealed"* believer. —JOHN MCNEIL

NOVEMBER 8

Be clothed with humility.
—1 Peter 5:5

Is it not one of the difficulties of church work that we have more officers than men? We need more of the rank and file, who are willing to march anywhere and do the lowliest of tasks. We will succeed in doing greater things when all are willing to be subjects. It is the bayonet rather than the gold braid that is needed when the enemy is to be subdued. —THOMAS CHAMPNESS

NOVEMBER 9

Examine yourselves.
—2 Corinthians 13:5

If your state be good, searching into it will give you that comfort of it. If your state be bad, searching into it cannot make it worse. Rather, it is the only way to make it better, for conversion begins with conviction. —BISHOP HOPKINS

NOVEMBER 10

*The pillar of the cloud went from before their face,
and stood behind them.*
—Exodus 14:19

It is not always guidance that we most need. Many of our dangers come upon us from behind. They are stealthy, insidious, assaulting us when we are unaware of their nearness. The tempter is cunning and shrewd. He does not meet us full front. It is a comfort to know that Christ comes behind us when it is there we need the protection.

—J. R. MILLER

NOVEMBER 11

*Iniquities prevail against me: as for our
transgressions, thou shalt purge them away.*
—Psalm 65:3

There is much earnest religion that lives in the dreary compass of these first four words, *"Iniquities prevail against me,"* and never gets a glimpse beyond it. But do not put a full stop there. Fetch in One who can help. "As for our transgressions, *You* shall purge them away." The moment we bring the Lord in, that moment defeat is turned to triumphant deliverance!

Write that up in golden letters, *You!* And do not find in this word only a trembling hope or a wondering wish. Listen to its full assurance, *You shall!* There is but one result that can warrant the agony of Calvary; there is but one result that can satisfy either our blessed Savior or ourselves; and that is our being conquerors over sin.

—MARK GUY PEARSE

NOVEMBER 12

Call to remembrance the former days.
—Hebrews 10:32

The former days—times of trial, conflict, discouragement, temptation. Did we oftener call these to remembrance; with how much more delight would we make the harbor of God's faithfulness our refuge, exclaiming with the psalmist, *"Because thou hast been my help, therefore in the shadow of thy wings will I rejoice"* (Psalm 63:7). —R. FULLER

NOVEMBER 13

In the world ye shall have tribulation: but be of good cheer; I have overcome the world.
—John 16:33

Tribulation is God's threshing—not to destroy us, but to get what is good, heavenly, and spiritual in us separated from what is wrong, earthly, and fleshly. Nothing less than blows of pain will do this. The evil clings so to the good, the golden wheat of goodness in us is so wrapped up in the strong chaff of the old life that only the heavy flail of suffering can produce the separation. —J. R. MILLER

NOVEMBER 14

Speaking the truth in love.
—Ephesians 4:15

The best way of eradicating error is to publish and practice truth. —W. ARNOT

NOVEMBER 15

They shall rejoice, and shall see the plummet in the hand of Zerubbabel.
—Zechariah 4:10

It is joy to the Christian to know that the plummet is now in the hands of our great Zerubbabel, and that when He comes forth, the world's misrule will be over. The false standards and false estimates of men will be swept away. The standards of expediency, of conscience, of every man thinking as he likes, if he is only sincere—these, and all similar refuges of lies will be like a spider's web. The measure of all things will be Christ, and Christ the Measurer of all things. How everything will be reversed! What a turning upside down of all that now exists!

Blessed and longed-for day, the world's great jubilee, the earth's long-sought Sabbath, groaning creation's joy, and nature's calm repose! Who would not cry, "Come, Lord Jesus, and end this troubled dream! Shatter the shadows of the long, dark night of sin and sorrow, sighing and tears, despair and death!" —F. WHITFIELD

NOVEMBER 16

And when the vessel that he made of the clay was
marred in the hand of the potter, he made it
again another vessel, as seemed good
to the potter to make it.
—Jeremiah 18:4 ASV

God's fairest, highest place of service in the land that lies beyond will be filled by the men and women who have been broken upon the wheel on earth. —G. CAMPBELL MORGAN

NOVEMBER 17

LORD, thou hast been our dwelling place
in all generations.
—Psalm 90:1

You cannot detain the eagle in the forest. You may gather around him a chorus of the choicest birds, you may give him a perch on the goodliest pine, you may charge winged messengers to bring him choicest dainties, but he will spurn them all. Spreading his lordly wings, and with his eyes on the alpine cliff, he will soar away to his own ancestral halls amid the munitions of rocks and the wild music of tempest and waterfall.

The soul of man, in its eagle soarings, will rest with nothing short of the Rock of Ages. Its ancestral halls are the halls of heaven. Its munitions of rocks are the attributes of God. The sweep of its majestic flight is eternity! "Lord, You have been our dwelling place in all generations!" —MACDUFF

NOVEMBER 18

So he arose and went to Zarephath.
—1 Kings 17:10

Let it be equally said of you to whatever duty the Lord may call you, *"He arose and went."* Be the way ever so laborious or dangerous, still arise, like Elijah, and go. Go cheerfully in faith, keeping your heart dependent on the Lord, and in the end you will surely behold His goodness. Though tossed on a sea of troubles, you may anchor on the firm, sure foundation of God. You have for security His exceeding precious promises, and may say with the psalmist, *"Why art thou cast down, O my soul? and why art thou disquieted within me? hope thou in God: for I shall yet praise him, who is the health of my countenance, and my God"* (Psalm 42:11).

—F. W. KRUMMACHER

NOVEMBER 19

He hath said.
—Hebrews 13:5

If we can only grasp these words of faith, we have an all-conquering weapon in our hand. What doubt is there that will not be slain by this two-edged sword? What fear is there that will not fall smitten with a deadly wound before this arrow from the bow of God's covenant? "He has said!" Yes, whether for delight in our quietude, or for strength in our conflict, "He has said!" must be our daily resort.

Since "He has said" is the source of all wisdom and the fountain of all comfort, let it dwell in you richly, as *"a well of water springing up into everlasting life"* (John 4:14). So you will grow healthy, strong, and happy, in the divine life.   —SPURGEON

NOVEMBER 20

Whom the Lord loveth he chasteneth.
—Hebrews 12:6

We should ever bear in mind that the discipline of our heavenly Father's hand is to be interpreted in the light of our Father's countenance, and the deep mysteries of His moral government are to be contemplated through the medium of His tender love.
—SELECTED

NOVEMBER 21

Who is my neighbour?
—Luke 10:29

"Who is my neighbour?" It is the sufferer, wherever, whoever, whatsoever he be. Wherever you hear the cry of distress, wherever you see anyone brought across your path by the chances and changes of life (that is, by the providence of God), whom it is in your power to help—stranger or enemy though he may be—he is your neighbor.
—A. P. STANLEY

NOVEMBER 22

Singing with grace in your hearts to the Lord.
—Colossians 3:16

Remember your life is to be a singing life. This world is God's grand cathedral for you. You are to be one of God's choristers, and there is to be a continual eucharistic sacrifice of praise and thanksgiving going up from your heart, with which God will be continually well pleased. And there should be not only the offering of the lips, but the surrender of the life with joy. Yes, with joy, and not with constraint. Every faculty of our nature should be presented to Him in gladsome service, for the Lord Jehovah is my song as well as my strength.

—W. HAY AITKEN

NOVEMBER 23

Jacob lifted up his eyes, and looked, and, behold, Esau came, and with him four hundred men.
—Genesis 33:1

Do not lift up your eyes and look for Esaus. Those who look for troubles will not be long without finding trouble to look at. Lift them higher—to Him from whom our help comes. Then you will be able to meet your troubles with an unperturbed spirit. Those who have seen the face of God need not fear the face of man that will die. To have power with God is to have power over all the evils that threaten us.

—F. B. MEYER

NOVEMBER 24

*I...heard behind me a great voice, as of a trumpet,
saying,...write.*
—Revelation 1:10–11

It is very sweet to note that a voice from heaven said to John, *"Write."* Does not that voice come to us? Are there not those who would taste the joys of heaven if we wrote them words of forgiveness and affection? Are there not others who would dry their tears if we would remind them of past joys, when we were poor as they are now? Could not some, who read these plain words, place inside the envelope something bearing their signature that would make the widow's heart dance for joy? What are our pens doing? Are they adding joy to other men's lives? If so, then angels may tune their harps when we sit at our desks. They are sent to minister to the heirs of salvation and would be glad to look upon our pens as writing music for them to sing, because what we write makes their client's joy to be full.

—THOMAS CHAMPNESS

NOVEMBER 25

Choose you this day whom ye will serve.
—Joshua 24:15

Choice and service—these were demanded of the Israelites; these are demanded of you, these only. Choice and service—in these are the whole of life.

—MARK HOPKINS

NOVEMBER 26

He touched the hollow of Jacob's thigh
in the sinew that shrank.
—Genesis 32:32

Whatever it is that enables a soul, whom God designs to bless, to stand out against Him, God will touch. It may be the pride of wealth, or of influence, or of affection, but it will not be spared—God will touch it. It may be something as natural as a sinew, but if it robs a man of spiritual blessing, God will touch it. It may be as small a thing as a sinew, but its influence in making a man strong in his resistance of blessing will be enough to condemn it, and God will touch it. Beneath that touch, it will shrink and shrivel, and you will limp to the end of life. Remember that the sinew never shrinks save beneath the touch of the angel hand—the touch of tender love.   —F. B. MEYER

NOVEMBER 27

Faithful is he that calleth you, who also will do it.
—1 Thessalonians 5:24

Earthly faithfulness is possible only by the reception of heavenly gifts. As surely as every leaf that grows is mainly water that the plant got from the clouds and carbon that it got from the atmosphere, so surely will all our good be mainly drawn from heaven and heaven's gifts. As certainly as every lump of coal that you put upon your fire contains in itself sunbeams that have been locked up for all these millenniums that have passed since it waved green in the forest, so certainly does every good deed embody in itself gifts from above. No man is pure except by impartation, and every good gift and every perfect gift comes from the Father of lights. (See James 1:17.)

—ALEXANDER MACLAREN

NOVEMBER 28

The LORD,...thy habitation.
—Psalm 91:9

We go home without arrangement. We plan our visits, and then go home because they are over. Duty, want, a host of things, lead us forth else-where, but the heart takes us home. Blessed, most blessed is he whose thoughts pass up to God, not because they are driven like a fisherman's craft swept by the fierceness of the storm, not because they are forced by want or fear, not because they are led by the hand of duty, but because God is in His habitation and His home. Loosed from other things, the thoughts go home for rest.

In God the blessed man finds the love that wel-comes. There is the sunny place. There, care is loosed and toil forgotten. There is the joyous free-dom, the happy calm, the rest, and renewing of our strength—at home with God. —MARK GUY PEARSE

NOVEMBER 29

With God all things are possible.
—Mark 10:27

Unbelief says, "How can such and such things be?" It is full of how's; but faith has one great answer to the ten thousand how's, and that answer is—God!
—C. H. M.

NOVEMBER 30

These...have turned the world upside down.
—Acts 17:6

None of these things move me.
—Acts 20:24

The men who move the world are the ones who do not let the world move them.
—AUTHOR UNKNOWN

DECEMBER

DECEMBER 1

A hearer of the word,...a doer of the work.
—James 1:23, 25

Religion may be learned on Sunday, but it is lived in the work of each weekday. The torch of religion may be lit in the church, but does its burning in the shop and on the street. Religion seeks its life in prayer, but lives its life in deeds. It is planted in the closet, but does its growing in the world. It plumes itself for flight in songs of praise, but its actual flights are in works of love. It resolves and meditates on faithfulness as it reads its Christian lesson in the Book of Truth, but "faithful is that faithful does." It puts its armor on with all the aids and helps of the sanctuary as its dressing room, but it combats for the right, the noble, and the good in all the activities of practical existence, and its battle ground is the whole broad field of life.

—JOHN DOUGHTY

DECEMBER 2

*Holy men of God spake as they were moved
by the Holy Ghost.*
—2 Peter 1:21

The Bible is the writing of the living God. Each letter was penned with an almighty finger. Each word in it dropped from the everlasting lips. Each sentence was dictated by the Holy Spirit. Granted that Moses was employed to write his histories with his fiery pen, but God guided that pen. It may be that David touched his harp and let sweet psalms of melody drop from his fingers, but God moved his hands over the living strings of his golden harp. Solomon sang canticles of love and gave forth words of consummate wisdom, but God directed his lips and made the preacher eloquent. If I follow the thundering Nahum when his horses plough the waters, or Habakkuk when he sees the tents of Cushan in affliction; if I read Malachi when the earth is burning like an oven; if I turn to the smooth page of John who tells of love, or the rugged chapters of Peter who speaks of fire devouring God's enemies; if I turn aside to Jude, who launches forth anathemas upon the foes of God, everywhere I find God speaking. It is God's voice, not man's: the words are God's words—the words of the Eternal, the Invisible, the Almighty, the Jehovah of ages. This Bible is God's Bible; and when I see it, I seem to hear a voice springing up from it, saying, "I am the Book of God. Man, read me. I am God's writing.

Study my pages, for I was penned by God. Love me, for He is my Author, and you will see Him visible and manifest everywhere." —SPURGEON

DECEMBER 3

When I am weak, then am I strong.
—2 Corinthians 12:10

This is God's way. We advance by going backward, we become strong by becoming weak, and we become wise by being fools. —F. WHITFIELD

DECEMBER 4

Belshazzar the king made a great feast.
—Daniel 5:1

There was one Guest not invited, but He came, and the work of His finger glowed upon the wall.
—SELECTED

DECEMBER 5

He that watereth shall be watered also himself.
—Proverbs 11:25

The effective life and the receptive life are one. There is no sweep of an arm that does some work for God, but it harvests also some more of the truth of God, and sweeps it into the treasury of life.
—PHILLIPS BROOKS

DECEMBER 6

Having therefore these promises.
—2 Corinthians 7:1

The forests in summer days are full of birds' nests, hidden among the leaves. The little birds know where they are. When a storm arises or when night draws on, they fly, each to his own nest. So the promises of God are hidden in the Bible, like nests in the great forests. There we should fly in any danger or alarm, hiding there in our soul's nest until the storm be past. There are no castles in this world so impregnable as the words of Christ.

—J. R. MILLER

DECEMBER 7

Bless the LORD, O my soul, and forget not all his benefits...who crowneth thee with lovingkindness and tender mercies.
—Psalm 103:2, 4

We talk about the telescope of faith, but I think we want even more the microscope of watchful and grateful love. Apply this to the little bits of our daily lives, in the light of the Spirit, and how wonderfully they will come out!   —FRANCES RIDLEY HAVERGAL

DECEMBER 8

Without Christ.
—Ephesians 2:12

Without a hope to cheer, a pilot to steer,
A friend to counsel, grace to sustain,
Heaven to welcome us, and God to console!
—AUTHOR UNKNOWN

DECEMBER 9

*God forbid that I should glory, save in the cross
of our Lord Jesus Christ.*
—Galatians 6:14

The cross is the great center of God's moral universe! To this center God ever pointed, and the eye of faith ever looked forward, until the Savior came. And now we must ever turn to that cross as the center of all our blessing, and the basis of all our worship, both on earth and in heaven, in time and throughout all eternity. —SELECTED

DECEMBER 10

He ever liveth.
—Hebrews 7:25

This is our hope for ourselves, and for His truth, and for mankind. Men come and go. Leaders, teachers, thinkers, all speak and work for a season, and then fall silent and impotent. He abides. They die, but He lives. They are lights kindled, and therefore sooner or later quenched, but He is the true Light from which they draw all their brightness, and He shines for forevermore. —ALEXANDER MACLAREN

DECEMBER 11

And they come unto him, bringing
one sick of the palsy.
—Mark 2:3

Had it not been for the palsy, this man might never have seen Christ!   —SELECTED

DECEMBER 12

Then shall ye...discern between
the righteous and the wicked.
—Malachi 3:18

Said Anne of Austria to Cardinal Richelieu: "God does not pay at the end of every week, but He pays at last!"

DECEMBER 13

Lot...pitched his tent toward Sodom.
—Genesis 13:12

And soon Lot moved into Sodom; and before long Sodom moved into him. —THEODORE CUYLER

DECEMBER 14

What is your life? It is even a vapour, that appeareth
for a little time, and then vanisheth away.
—James 4:14

Only one life; 'twill soon be past,
And only what's done for Christ will last.
—SELECTED

DECEMBER 15

Cleanse thou me from secret faults.
—Psalm 19:12

Most men are free from gross, public faults. The world needs men who are free from secret faults.
—SELECTED

DECEMBER 16

*When thou passest through the waters,
I will be with thee.*
—Isaiah 43:2

God's presence in the trial is much better than exemption from the trial. The sympathy of His heart with us is far sweeter than the power of His hand for us. —AUTHOR UNKNOWN

DECEMBER 17

Now abideth faith, hope, love, these three; but the greatest of these is love.
—1 Corinthians 13:13 ASV

Love is the greatest thing that God can give us, for He Himself is Love. It is the greatest thing we can give to God, for it will give ourselves, and carry with it all that is ours. —JEREMY TAYLOR

DECEMBER 18

Go and sit down in the lowest room.
—Luke 14:10

He who is willing to take the lowest place will always find sitting room; there is no great crush for the worst places. There is nothing like the jostling at the back that there is at the front. So if we would be comfortable, we would do well to keep behind.

—THOMAS CHAMPNESS

DECEMBER 19

The disciples were called Christians first in Antioch.
—Acts 11:26

This name suggests that the clear impression made by our character, as well as by our words, should be that we belong to Jesus Christ. He should manifestly be the center and the guide, the impulse and the pattern, the strength and reward of our lives. We are Christians. That should be plain for all folks to see, whether we speak or be silent. Is it so with you? —ALEXANDER MACLAREN

DECEMBER 20

They all forsook him, and fled.
—Mark 14:50

Separation never comes from His side.

—J. HUDSON TAYLOR

DECEMBER 21

He [Jesus] *looked up to heaven.*
—Mark 6:41

In working for God, first look to heaven. It is a grand plan. Over and over again our Lord Jesus Christ looked to heaven and said, *"Father."* Let us imitate Him. Although standing on the earth, let us have our conversation in heaven. Before you go out, if you would feed the world, if you would be a blessing in the midst of spiritual death and famine, lift up your head to heaven. Then your very face will shine, your very garments will smell of myrrh and aloes and cassia out of the ivory palaces where you have been with your God and Savior. There will be stamped upon you the dignity and power of the service of the Most High God.   —MCNEIL

DECEMBER 22

The friendship of the world is enmity with God.
—James 4:4

It is like the ivy with the oak. The ivy may give the oak a grand, beautiful appearance, but all the while it is feeding on its vitals. Are we compromising with the enemies of God? Are we being embraced by the world by its honors, its pleasures, its applause? This may add to us in the world's estimation, but our strength becomes lost.
—DENHAM SMITH

DECEMBER 23

She [Hannah]...*prayed unto the* Lord, *and wept sore....*
She spake in her heart.
—1 Samuel 1:10, 13

For real business at the mercy seat give me a homemade prayer, a prayer that comes out of the depths of my heart, not because I invented it, but because God the Holy Spirit put it there, and gave it such living force that I could not help letting it out. Though your words are broken, and your sentences disconnected, if your desires are earnest, if they are like coals of juniper, burning with a vehement flame, God will not mind how they are expressed. If you have no words, perhaps you will pray better without them than with them. There are prayers that break the backs of words: they are too heavy for any human language to carry. —SPURGEON

DECEMBER 24

Behold, I bring you good tidings of great joy,
which shall be to all people.
—Luke 2:10

It is true that these good tidings of great joy were to be *"to all people,"* but not at first. The message falls on our own ears and is first for our own souls.

Oh, ponder this well! Take God's truths home first to your own heart. Ask in earnest prayer that the Spirit may write them with a pen of heaven on your conscience. Then will you be a vessel fitted for the Master's use to carry His message with spiritual power to others. —F. WHITFIELD

DECEMBER 25

A multitude of the heavenly host praising God, and
saying, Glory to God in the highest.
—Luke 2:13–14

Angels had been present on many august occasions, and they had joined in many a solemn chorus to the praise of their Almighty Creator. They were present at the creation: *"The morning stars sang together, and all the sons of God shouted for joy"* (Job 38:7). They had seen planets fashioned between the palms of Jehovah and wheeled by His eternal hands through the infinitude of space. They had sung solemn songs over many a world that the Great One had created. We do not doubt that they had often chanted, "Blessing and honor, and glory, and majesty, and power, and dominion, and might, be unto him that sits on the throne," manifesting Himself in the work of creation. I doubt not, too, that their songs had gathered force through the ages. As when first created, their first breath was song, so when they saw God create new worlds, then their song received another note; they rose a little higher in the gamut of adoration. But this time, when they saw God stoop from His throne and become a babe sleeping upon a woman's breast, they lifted their notes higher still; reaching to the uttermost stretch of angelic music, they gained the highest notes of the divine scale of praise and sang, *"Glory to God in the highest,"* for higher in goodness they felt God could not go. Thus their highest praise they gave to Him in the highest act of His Godhead.   —SPURGEON

DECEMBER 26

Which hope we have as an anchor of the soul.
—Hebrews 6:19

Anchor to the throne of God, and then shorten the rope! —SELECTED

DECEMBER 27

Noah found grace in the eyes of the LORD.
—Genesis 6:8

Noah found grace in the same way that Paul obtained mercy (see 1 Timothy 1:16)—namely, by mercy's taking hold of him. —SELECTED

DECEMBER 28

The sea wrought, and was tempestuous.
—Jonah 1:11

Sin in the soul is like Jonah in the ship. It turns the smoothest water into a wild, tempestuous sea. —SELECTED

DECEMBER 29

Be not slothful, but followers of them who through faith and patience inherit the promises.
—Hebrews 6:12

God makes a promise. Faith believes it. Hope anticipates it. Patience quietly awaits it. —SELECTED

DECEMBER 30

Ye know not what shall be on the morrow.
—James 4:14

Tomorrow is the devil's great ally—the very Goliath in whom he trusts for victory. *Now* is the stripling sent forth against him. The world will freely agree to be Christians tomorrow if Christ will permit them to be worldly today.

—WILLIAM ARNOT

DECEMBER 31

He [Thomas] *said,....Except I shall see...I will not believe....*[Jesus] *saith...be not faithless, but believing.*
—John 20:25, 27

Every doubt in the heart of a Christian is a dishonor done to the Word of God and the sacrifice of Christ. —SELECTED

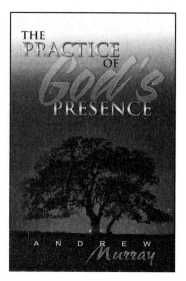

The Practice of God's Presence
Andrew Murray

Is something missing in your Christian life? Do you long to become the person God wants you to be, to feel His presence and experience His power? Andrew Murray's scriptural insights make it easy for you to know God. Learn how to have a dynamic, joy-filled relationship with the Lord. Live every day, every hour, in intimate fellowship with Him. In this collection of six of Murray's best-sellers, you will discover that not only can you have an effective prayer life, but you can also experience the fullness of the Holy Spirit, a blameless heart, and victory over sin.

ISBN: 0-88368-590-6 • Trade • 576 pages

W

WHITAKER
HOUSE

proclaiming the power of the Gospel through the written word
visit our website at www.whitakerhouse.com

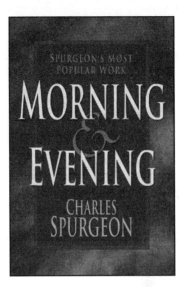

Morning and Evening
(revised version)
Charles H. Spurgeon

"Encouraging thoughts are like honey to the heart," wrote
Charles Spurgeon, whose uplifting messages for each day
of the year will bring comfort and refreshment to your
walk with God. Whether you spend your time alone with
God in the morning or evening or both, Spurgeon's rich
biblical insights, extraordinary eloquence, and clarity
of logic will powerfully affect your faith and
enhance your intimacy with the Lord.

ISBN: 0-88368-749-6 • Trade • 752 pages

W
WHITAKER
HOUSE

proclaiming the power of the Gospel through the written word
visit our website at www.whitakerhouse.com

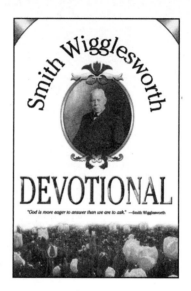

Smith Wigglesworth Devotional
Smith Wigglesworth

You are invited to journey with Smith Wigglesworth on a
year-long trip that will quench your spiritual thirst while
it radically transforms your faith. As you daily explore
these challenging insights from the Apostle of Faith, you
will connect with God's glorious power, cast out doubt,
and see impossibilities turn into realities. Your prayer
life will never be the same again when you personally
experience the joy of seeing awesome, powerful results
as you extend God's healing grace to others.

ISBN: 0-88368-574-4 • Trade • 560 pages

ധ
WHITAKER
HOUSE

proclaiming the power of the Gospel through the written word
visit our website at www.whitakerhouse.com